# ...WHO NEEDS THEM?...

# ...WHO NEEDS THEM?...

*LIN JOHNSON*

VICTOR BOOKS®
A DIVISION OF SCRIPTURE PRESS PUBLICATIONS INC.
USA CANADA ENGLAND

**More Young Teen Feedback Electives**

*The School Zone*
*Nobody Like Me*
*For Real People Only*
*What's Your Problem*
*Family Survival Guide*



ISBN: 0-89693-610-4


Printed in the United States of America.

# CONTENTS

INTRODUCTION **7**

## *I. FRIENDS—WHO ARE THEY?* 9

Session 1 **THE BEST OF FRIENDS 11**
Biblical examples of friendships teach us qualities to imitate.

Session 2 **FOLLOW THAT FRIEND 17**
How Jesus treated people shows us how to be friends.

Session 3 **WHAT KIND OF FRIEND ARE YOU? 21**
We can become better friends by comparing ourselves to biblical qualities for a friend.

Session 4 **MEASURING UP ON THE FRIENDSHIP SCALE 25**
Paul's description of love also describes a true friend.

## *II. FRIENDS—HOW DO THEY ACT?* 29

Session 5 **SPEAKING OF FRIENDSHIP 31**
A key friendship skill is knowing how to ask questions.

Session 6 **IS ANYBODY OUT THERE LISTENING? 37**
Friends learn to listen to others.

Session 7 **A FRIEND IN DEED 43**
To have friends we must reach out to others.

Session 8 **BUILDING BRIDGES 49**
Evangelism begins by sharing ourselves and our faith with our non-Christian friends.

## *III. FRIENDS—OVERCOMING OBSTACLES* 55

Session 9 **SQUEEZED FROM ALL SIDES 57**
We don't have to give in to the pressures of friends.

Session 10 **POPULARITY PROFILE 63**
Popularity is achieved by putting other people first.

Session 11 **CLIMBING THE WALLS 69**
We need to identify and overcome barriers to friendships.

Session 12 **WHEN FRIENDS FIGHT 73**
Conflicts don't have to break up friendships.

*FRIENDS: WHO NEEDS THEM?* is designed to help your young teens appropriate biblical qualities of a friend, develop friendship skills, and overcome problems in friendships. As part of the Young Teen Feedback Elective series, this book presents creative Bible studies that will keep your young teens interested and challenge them to spiritual growth.

## *HOW TO USE YOUNG TEEN FEEDBACK ELECTIVES*

You'll discover that these studies are especially geared toward young teens—a group in the midst of change. As they struggle to make the transition from children to adults, young teens show extremes of behavior—energetic one minute, withdrawn the next. These fast-paced studies offer a variety of teaching methods to appeal to these sometimes hard-to-interest group members. Each creative session is firmly founded on the Word of God.

Each lesson focuses on one or more Bible truths that can be applied directly to young teens' lives. Make sure you have enough Bibles so that students who forget theirs can borrow them. Try to have some modern-language translations on hand for easy comprehension.

If you're unfamiliar with Young Teen Feedback Electives, take a few minutes to study this overview of your elective study.

**Flexible Format**
Notice that you can study the topic of this book over a 12-week quarter. In addition, each subtopic is complete in itself, so you can study part of this elective for four weeks, returning to the other studies at a later time. This format gives you flexibility to suit your program to the particular needs of your young people. It also lets you tailor the study to your schedule.

**Introductory Page**
Each session has an easy-to-use summary of the lesson on the first page to help you see the lesson at a glance.

- *Key Concept* clearly states the lesson's theme.
- *Meeting the Need* outlines general concerns and questions young teens have on the session's subject. By understanding their concerns, you can better help teens apply the lesson.
- *Session Goals* includes the objectives of the lesson in measurable terms. Each goal helps communicate the Key Concept and should be achieved by group members by the end of the session.
- *Special Preparation* gives you a checklist of what you'll need to lead the session.

**Building the Body**
The first minutes of each session are devoted to relationship building. These exercises, activities, and optional "warm-ups" will help your group get to know one another and you—a key to an open group where good Bible study can take place. These activities also provide a transition time which takes young teens away from outside concerns and points

them toward the group study.

**Launching the Lesson**
This section offers focus discussions and activities that zero in on needs and interests that will be covered by the Bible study later in the lesson.

**Exploring the Word**
This part of the study contains creative ways to communicate Bible truths and concepts. It not only helps *you* share God's Word, but it also allows young teens to discover God's Word for themselves.

**Applying the Truth**
This application section summarizes Bible truths and concepts. It helps young teens relate Christian faith and values to their everyday lives, answering the question, "What does this mean to me?"

**Workout Sheets**
These activity sheets encourage young teens to discover concepts, facts, and ideas in a variety of ways. The sheets are meant to be reproduced. Just tear out the master copy and make as many duplicates as you need. You may want to provide folders for group members to collect and save their Workout Sheets.

**Student Books**
Student books are available to help bring home Bible truths to young teens in your group. These lively books are written by men and women who know how to communicate to your young people. They can be used many different ways:

■ Have group members read the chapter *after* each session so material covered in class will be reinforced and "come alive" at home.

■ Have group members read a chapter *before* each session to stimulate their thinking on the subject and get them ready for in-class discussions.

■ Use portions of the books *during* the group study. For instance, incorporate a case study from the book into a group discussion.

You can complete this elective study without using the student books, but we recommend them as an excellent tool to give students their own version of the material you study together. It's something permanent that they can refer to long after the group study has ended. These books are entertaining, informative, and fun to use. Their small size makes them portable; they fit easily into pockets or purses. Look for them at your local Christian bookstore, and add them to this elective study.

**Before Each Lesson**
Pray for your young teens as they work through this study. Ask the Lord to help you create an open atmosphere in your group, so that teens will feel free to share with each other and you.

**After Each Lesson**
Evaluate each session as you ask yourself the following questions: Did each student achieve the lesson goals? Why or why not? Did you have the right amount of time to complete the lesson? How many group members actively took part in the session? Are interpersonal relationships being nurtured in the group? How well did you prepare the lesson? How might you change your presentation next time?

# PART ONE

## ...WHO ARE THEY?

Young teens crave friends. They want and need buddies to hang around with, special friends to share secrets with, and lots of people to talk and do things with. But many of them do not know how to be this kind of friend to others. They just assume that no matter how they act their peers will want to be friends. And when some of them don't, they are disappointed, hurt, frustrated, and sometimes angry.

The young teen years are a prime time to learn how to be better friends. Social relationships are becoming more important as they move out of the gang stage and begin to seek independence from their parents and other family members.

In this first section on friendship, you will guide your group members to develop qualities which will attract other people and help them to be the kind of friends they—and others—want. To do this, you will inspect selected biblical friendships; watch the ideal friend, Jesus Christ, in action; study God's instructions pertaining to friends; and evaluate your own lives. Along the way, you will encourage your young teens to begin to practice these qualities in order to make them part of their lifestyles.

# FRIENDS — WHO ARE THEY?

*SESSION 1*

## *THE BEST OF FRIENDS*

**KEY CONCEPT**

Biblical examples of friendships teach us qualities to imitate.

**MEETING THE NEED**

This session will respond to the following student questions and comments:

- "How can I show someone I want to be his or her friend?"
- "The best thing a friend can do for me is help me."
- "I look for friends who like me for who I am."

**SESSION GOALS**

You will help each group member

1. identify ways we show friendship,
2. discover how selected Bible people demonstrated friendship,
3. select one Bible person to emulate and list ways to follow his example.

**SPECIAL PREPARATION**

____ If you use "Bible Pairs," write the names of each half of a Bible pair on slips of paper. Be certain you have enough pairs for the size of your group plus a few extra for visitors.
____ For "Friends Charades" write both names of each media pair of friends on the same slip of paper. Choose a few more pairs than the number of your group.
____ Box for "Building the Body" activities
____ Envelopes, one per group member
____ List ways young teens can follow the examples of the Bible friends they will study in this session.

# BUILDING THE BODY

Use one or both of these activities to get this session off to an active start.

## *BIBLE PAIRS*

As group members arrive, have each one draw out of a box the name of half of a Bible pair. Do not put all of the pairs in the box at once in case you have more pairs than students; add names as you need to. Instruct group members not to tell anyone who they drew.

When it is time to start, have group members try to find their partners by asking questions without using the name of either half of the pair. Choose pairs with which your group is most familiar. Some suggested pairs are:

Adam and Eve
Cain and Abel
Jacob and Esau
Abraham and Sarah
Moses and Aaron
Deborah and Barak
David and Jonathan
Ruth and Naomi
Elijah and Elisha
Peter and Andrew
Paul and Barnabas
Priscilla and Aquila
James and John
Mary and Martha
Samson and Delilah
Ahab and Jezebel
Mary and Joseph
Ananias and Sapphira

## *FRIENDS CHARADES*

Instruct group members to stand in two equal lines and count off, each line starting with 1. Then have the same numbers pair off; i.e., the "1s" become a pair, the "2s" become a pair. (If you have an odd number of young teens, have them form one triad.) Let each pair draw the names of famous media friends. Instruct them to quietly and briefly consult on how to show who they are without talking.

Have each pair take turns in acting out who they are while the rest of the group tries to guess their identities.

Choose pairs with which your group members are familiar. Use the following suggestions, adding any others you can think of.

Abbott and Costello
Cagney and Lacey
LaVerne and Shirley
Hansel and Gretel
Romeo and Juliet
Simon and Simon
Holmes and Watson
Kate and Allie
Tom and Jerry
Popeye and Olive Oyl
Bert and Ernie
Hawkeye and B.J.
Lone Ranger and Tonto
Charlie Brown and Snoopy
Roy Rogers and Trigger
Ralph Cramden and Ed Norton
Mickey Mouse and Donald Duck
Captain Kirk and Mr. Spock

# LAUNCHING THE LESSON

## CIRCLE CONVERSATION

Ask: **What are some ways we show that we are friends with another person?** Go around the group and have everyone tell one way without repeating any. If your group is large, ask for volunteers to answer the question.

Explain that during this session you will look at some Bible people and how they demonstrated friendship to others.

# EXPLORING THE WORD

## STUDENT BOOK OPTION

Use the story about the Friends Factory Outlet in chapter 1 of the student book to introduce the Bible friends you will study. You may ask three good readers to read the story aloud, each taking one part. Or you may want to contact three group members during the week and ask them to prepare to act out the story.

## FRIENDS FACTORY OUTLET

If you aren't using the student books, read or tell this story to your group members:

**Kevin looked up at the sign. "Friends Factory Outlet" it proclaimed in large letters.**

**"This is the place," Kevin said to Tom, as he turned to enter the store. A bell announced their arrival when he opened the door.**

**Immediately a smiling salesman greeted them. "Welcome to Friends Factory Outlet. I'm your *friendly* salesman. How may I help you?" he asked.**

**"We're looking for some models to take to our youth group at church."**

**"I see," the salesman replied, still smiling broadly. "We have a number of models you might be interested in. Right this way, please."**

**Kevin and Tom followed the salesman over to the left wall of the store. On the way they eyed a number of interesting-looking figures.**

**The salesman stopped and pointed to a handsome pair. "These are our most popular models, Dave and Jon. They are loyal to each other at all costs. Jon, especially, is outstanding in the loyalty de-**

partment, more so than any other model we stock."

Kevin looked at Tom. "Well, we *are* short of loyalty in our group. I can't remember the last time someone stuck up for another group member. I guess we should take them." Tom nodded his approval.

"Good choice," the salesman said. "But we do have several more I'd like to show you." He gestured to a pair across the aisle.

"The one on the left looks kind of old," Tom remarked.

"Don't let his age fool you," the salesman countered. "Paul is one of our most famous models. Why, he's been written up in more books and magazines than any other figure we stock!

"He comes in a variety of ages, but most people prefer this older one, particularly if they take Tim along with him. The two of them are excellent examples of getting along together and of encouraging each other."

Tom turned to Kevin. "We certainly could use more friendships like that. It seems like everyone is criticizing someone else. Let's take them too."

"OK," Kevin agreed. "Add them to our order."

"My friend," said the salesman, "you'll be glad you did. Now let me give you some *friendly* advice and show you one more model. He's been reduced for quick sale. Most people don't think of him as belonging in the Friends Factory, but he is a definite asset to our line of models."

The salesman walked briskly toward the back of the store. Tom and Kevin followed at a slower pace, pausing to look at a number of figures and to read the hangtags. The salesman waited patiently for them to catch up.

"This is Sam," he announced as he pointed proudly at a model who looked a little out of place.

"He doesn't look like the rest," Kevin remarked.

"That's right, but that difference is what makes him an *excellent* model. Sam can teach your youth group a lot about helping other people, especially those who are different from you."

Kevin and Tom looked at each other. "We'll take him," they said at the same time.

"Our leaders are always telling us we should be more helpful," Kevin added. "But nobody's listening."

"Would you like to look at any more today?" asked the salesman.

"I think we have enough for a while," Kevin answered. "How soon can we expect delivery?"

**"I'll have to check our stock on the computer. Let's go over to the sales counter." The salesman led the way to the center of the store. He punched in the codes for each model, then turned to Kevin and Tom. "I'm sorry, but the models you've chosen are all on back order. We're expecting a shipment in about two weeks. Let me write up your order, and then I'll give you a facts sheet which you can study in the meantime.**

Say: **Let's look more closely at the fact sheet on the friend models Kevin and Tom picked out for their group.**

## *WORKOUT SHEET*

Divide group members into three study groups. Give each group a copy of Workout Sheet #1, "Friends Factory Outlet Fact Sheet," and a pencil. Appoint group leaders, and assign one of the friendship models to each group. If your group is large, divide members into six study groups and assign each study to two groups. Instruct the groups to read their Scripture passages, list what they learn about building friendships, and then list specific ways they can follow these examples today.

Reassemble the group. Call for reports on the friendship builders, and list them on the left side of the chalkboard or an overhead transparency. (You will discuss ways to follow these examples later in the session.) Use the following information to supplement group reports.

**Group 1—Jonathan and David** (1 Samuel 18:1-4; 19:1-7; 23:15-18)
Friendship builders:
- Love your friend.
- Be committed to each other.
- Help your friend.
- Say good things about your friend.
- Seek out the other person; don't wait for him to come to you.
- Encourage your friend in God.
- Help him to follow God.

**Group 2—Paul and Timothy** (Philippians 2:19-24; 2 Timothy 1:3-8)
Friendship builders:
- Have common interests.
- Serve God together.
- Be trustworthy, dependable.
- Pray for your friend.
- Encourage your friend to grow spiritually.

**Group 3—Good Samaritan** (Luke 10:30-37)
Friendship builders:
- Notice other people.
- Feel compassion for others. (Compassion is sympathy plus action to help.)
- Take time to help others.
- Use what resources you have to help others.

### DISCUSSION

Have students look over the list of friendship builders. **Which ones hadn't you thought about as ways to be friends? Why?**

# APPLYING THE TRUTH

### REPORTS

Ask each group to report their suggestions for following these friendship builders today. List them on the right side of the board or transparency. Suggestions might include: sending a birthday card, cheering up a friend, not criticizing or making fun of a friend, sticking up for him when others say bad things about him, helping him with chores or school work he doesn't understand, calling him, praying for him, doing a Bible study together, sharing a hobby, keeping promises, encouraging each other to follow through on Sunday School and youth group assignments, mowing the lawn or shoveling snow for a neighbor or widow, talking to and eating with classmates who are ignored by others. As you have time, ask for suggestions from other group members.

### WORKOUT SHEET

Distribute copies of Workout Sheet #2, "A Letter to Myself," envelopes, and pencils. Instruct each group member to complete the letter, seal it in the envelope, and address the envelope to himself. Explain that you will return the letters next week so group members can evaluate how well they did during the week. Collect the envelopes.

### PRAYER

Close with a few minutes of sentence prayers, focusing on asking God to help them become more like their chosen Bible friend.

**JONATHAN AND DAVID**

PASSAGES: 1 Samuel 18:1-4; 19:1-7; 23:15-18

BACKGROUND: Jonathan was King Saul's son. Normally, he would have become king when Saul died, but God chose David to become king instead.

**PAUL AND TIMOTHY**

PASSAGES: Philippians 2:19-24; 2 Timothy 1:3-8

**GOOD SAMARITAN**

PASSAGE: Luke 10:30-37

***WAYS THEY DEMONSTRATED FRIENDSHIP:***

______________________________

______________________________

______________________________

______________________________

______________________________

***WAYS WE CAN FOLLOW THEIR EXAMPLES:***

______________________________

______________________________

______________________________

______________________________

______________________________

# A letter to Myself

Dear Me,
Today I learned how some Bible people built friendships. The biblical friend I want to become more like is ____________________
because:

I can follow his example by:

Yours truly,
Me

# FRIENDS — WHO ARE THEY?

*SESSION 2*

## *FOLLOW THAT FRIEND*

**KEY CONCEPT**

How Jesus treated people shows us how to be friends.

**MEETING THE NEED**

This session will respond to the following student questions and comments:

- "Why should I be friends with him? He never sticks up for me."
- "My mom wants me to be friends with her friend's daughter since we're the same age, but she's a geek."
- "I think a good friend is someone who likes me for myself."

**SESSION GOALS**

You will help each group member

1. define or describe an ideal friend,
2. discover what several of Jesus' friends were like and how He treated them,
3. discuss ways to be a friend like Jesus and choose one to practice this week.

**SPECIAL PREPARATION**

____ Bring notebook paper and safety pins, enough for everyone.

____ Make an overhead transparency of Workout Sheet #3, omitting the instructions, and bring a marking pen. Or plan to write it on the chalkboard. Add to the descriptions given in the example in "Launching the Lesson."

____ Write the Bible study assignments on separate sheets of paper. Collect four manners and customs books, Bible dictionaries, or encyclopedias which provide the information group members must look up. A Bible handbook is the best source of information about the prostitute in Luke 7.

# BUILDING THE BODY

Use one or both of the following activities to affirm your group members.

### *FRIEND BOMBING*

Arrange the chairs in a circle, putting one in the middle. Or have group members sit on the floor in a circle. One-by-one call each group member to sit in the middle. Have the group members in the circle take turns completing this statement: **You make a good friend because you ______.** Encourage group members to be as specific as possible in their statements.

If you think some group members will find this activity uncomfortable, try this variation: Have two or three volunteers complete the statement for the person in the middle.

When everyone has been affirmed, ask group members how they felt to have someone tell them they are good friends.



### *GOOD FRIEND LISTS*

Pin a sheet of notebook paper on everyone's back, and give each person a pencil. Instruct group members to write one thing they like about each person on his or her list. Emphasize that comments must be positive.

When the lists are completed, instruct group members to help each other remove the lists from their backs. Allow time for individuals to read them silently. Then discuss how they felt when they read the comments.

# LAUNCHING THE LESSON

### *WORKOUT SHEET*

Distribute Workout Sheet #3, "How Do You Spell Friend?" and pencils. Instruct group members to define or describe an ideal friend with words or short phrases that begin with those letters. Let them work individually or in pairs. (If your group enjoys a challenge, set a time limit and see who can come up with the most words or phrases.) Then record responses on an overhead transparency or the chalkboard. (Save for use at the end of the session.) For example,

**F** orgiving
**R** espectful
**I** s kind
**E** ncouraging
**N** ice
**D** ependable

Say something like: **The ideal is seldom seen in real life, but there *is* one person who fits our description—Jesus Christ. Let's look at**

**several of His friendships to see how He demonstrated these qualities.**

# EXPLORING THE WORD

## *BIBLE STUDY*

Divide group members into four study groups, appoint leaders, and give each group a reference book and a sheet of paper with one of the following assignments:

**Group 1—Unnamed woman and Simon** (Treat each person separately.)
*Luke 7:36-50*
Look up this passage in the Bible handbook to find out what kind of woman she was. Also find out what Pharisees were like.

**Group 2—Zaccheus**
*Luke 19:1-10*
Find out what tax collectors were like.

**Group 3—Peter**
*Matthew 4:18-20; John 13:1-5; Matthew 26:69-75*
Find out whose job it was to wash the guests' feet and why.

**Group 4—Judas**
*John 12:4-6; Matthew 26:14-16; John 13:21-26; Matthew 26:47-50*
Look up the meaning of giving the morsel of bread.

Explain how to use the reference books you have brought, pointing out the Scripture index in the manners and customs books. Or to save time, give each group a book with the appropriate page(s) marked.

Have each group read their passage(s) and answer these two questions:

- **What was Jesus' friend like?**
- **How did Jesus treat this friend?**

After about 15 minutes, reassemble the group and call for reports. Use the commentary which follows to supplement as necessary.

**Group 1—Unnamed woman and Simon**
The woman was a prostitute who took a risk in going to a Pharisee's house to meet Jesus. Because she washed His feet with her tears and hair, she must have loved Him a great deal, a demonstration of her faith in Him. Jesus did not push her away, but accepted her and forgave her sins.

Simon was a Pharisee, one of the religious leaders who kept the letter of the law. He condemned the woman and her actions. Jesus taught him truth through a story, pointing out his sin of condemnation.

**Group 2—Zaccheus**
Zaccheus collected taxes for the hated Roman government and there-

fore was despised by the Jewish people. He was wealthy because he cheated people by charging more than they owed and kept the excess. Thus, the people considered him a sinner. He was determined to see Jesus. Jesus noticed him and spent time with him. As a result, Zaccheus repented of his sin and determined to make restitution to those he had cheated.

**Group 3—Peter**
Peter was a fisherman who followed Jesus without hesitation. When Jesus called him in Matthew 4, Peter had probably met and heard Him speak before. He denied Jesus three times but repented, as evidenced by his weeping. Jesus called Peter to obedience to Himself. By washing the disciples' feet, He willingly served them by doing an unpleasant job usually performed by a household servant. He demonstrated great love to Peter and the other disciples.

**Group 4—Judas**
Judas, one of Jesus' chosen twelve disciples, was the group's treasurer and a thief. He betrayed Jesus to the religious leaders in exchange for money. Even though Jesus knew Judas would betray Him shortly, He gave him a dipped piece of bread at the Passover meal which signified a special friendship, showing him love. While Judas was betraying Him, Jesus still called him a friend.



### *DISCUSSION*

Discuss together: **Why was Jesus a good friend?** Include some of the examples from the student book.

Show the FRIEND acrostic again; or if you put it on the chalkboard, direct group members' attention to it. Ask: **How did Jesus demonstrate these qualities of a friend?**

# APPLYING THE TRUTH

### *WORKOUT SHEET*

Distribute Workout Sheet #4, "Follow That Friend," and have everyone form pairs or triads, depending on the size of your group. Ask them to write down the quality of friendship they find most important. Or assign one quality of a good friend from the acrostic or the Bible study to each pair, instructing them to write it at the top of the Workout Sheet. Give them 3-5 minutes to list or draw specific ways young teens could demonstrate that quality in their schools, neighborhoods, or church group. Then have each pair report their suggestions. Help your group members understand that they can follow Jesus' example of a friend today.

Instruct everyone to choose one way they will be a friend like Jesus this week and record their decisions on the bottom of the Workout Sheet.

Close with a few minutes of sentence prayers, asking God to help them be the kind of friend Jesus is in the ways they wrote down.

# HOW DO YOU SPELL

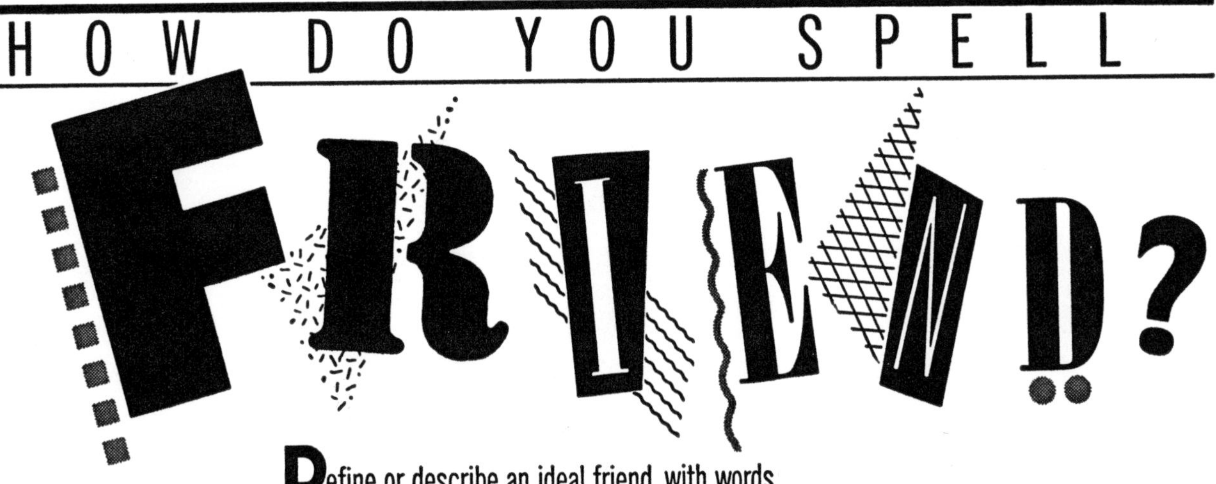


Define or describe an ideal friend with words or short phrases which begin with the following letters. You may have more than one description for each letter.

F

R

I

E

N

D

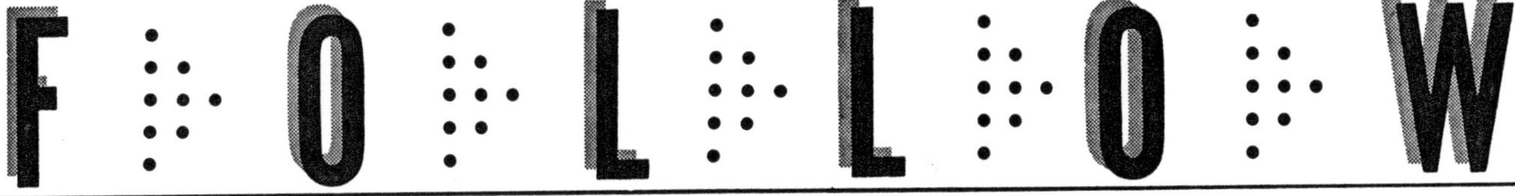


# FOLLOW THAT FRIEND

▶ *What quality in a friend is most important to you?*

▶ *Why?*

▶ *List or draw cartoons of specific ways you and your friends could demonstrate that quality in your own lives at:*

SCHOOL

HOME

CHURCH

Are you willing to follow the all-time best Friend, Jesus?
If you want to practice the friendship-style of Jesus, fill out and sign the pledge below.

## PLEDGE

*I want to be a friend like Jesus this week. Therefore, I will (write one action you plan to take):*

______________________________

______________________________.

______________________________
*Signature*

## SESSION 3

# WHAT KIND OF FRIEND ARE YOU?

**KEY CONCEPT**

Comparing ourselves to biblical qualities of a friend challenges us to become better friends.

**MEETING THE NEED**

This session will respond to the following student questions and comments:
- "Why don't people like me?"
- "I try to be a friend, but it doesn't always work."
- "He sure wasn't my friend for very long."

**SESSION GOALS**

You will help each group member
1. illustrate qualities they like in friends,
2. identify biblical qualities of a friend,
3. choose one quality he is lacking in and list steps to develop it.

**SPECIAL PREPARATION**

____ Collect the following items for "Friendship Symbols": large paper bags, construction paper, aluminum foil, chenille wires, transparent tape, safety pins, scissors, marking pens.
____ If you decide to do the "Friendship Symbols," make a sample; i.e., a clock to represent the fact that friends spend time together.
____ Gather 3′ lengths of shelf paper, old magazines with pictures, scissors, rubber cement, tables (optional), masking tape.
____ Locate a tape with the song "Friends" by Michael W. Smith (on the tape *Michael W. Smith Project*), and bring a cassette player (optional).

# BUILDING THE BODY

Start your session with one or both of the following activities to help your group members begin to think about qualities they like in friends.

### HUMAN SCULPTURES

Divide the group into two or four teams. Allow about 10 minutes for the groups to huddle and choose body positions to illustrate qualities they like in their friends. They may pose as individuals or pairs.

When time is up, have one team get in their positions while the other team tries to guess the qualities. (If using four teams, have two posing at the same time, assigning one team each to guess qualities.) Keep score of correct guesses. Then switch teams.

Summarize the qualities that have been exhibited, commenting on the diversity of what we appreciate in friends.



### FRIENDSHIP SYMBOLS

Put the following items in large paper bags, one bag for every six to eight group members: construction paper, scissors, aluminum foil, chenille wires, safety pins (one per person), marking pens, transparent tape.

Divide group members into small groups, and give each group a paper bag. Tell them they have 10 minutes to each design a symbol of friendship. Show your sample.

When time is up, have each person pin his symbol on someone else, explaining what it is if necessary.

If you have time, have everyone show and tell the symbol he was given or ask for volunteers to do so. Summarize briefly the qualities we look for in friends.

# LAUNCHING THE LESSON

### MONTAGES

(If you omit "Building the Body" activities, begin the montages as group members arrive. Plan to have four to six people make a montage.)

Direct group members to a table or section of the floor with materials for making a montage. Instruct them to cut or tear out from the magazines words and pictures to illustrate characteristics of a good friend and then glue them on the long sheet of paper.

After about 10 minutes, have each group tape their montage on the wall and briefly explain the items on it.

Comment on how important these characteristics are in the friends we choose. Point out that other people are looking for the same qualities in us. Then mention that God gives us guidelines in His Word for what a friend should be like.

# EXPLORING THE WORD

## *WORKOUT SHEET*

To discover biblical qualities of friends, distribute copies of Workout Sheet #5, "Friendly Finds," and pencils. Have students read each verse and complete the statement, "A Friend ______" with the quality that each verse mentions. You may want to assign each verse to an individual, pair, or small group instead of having everyone study all the verses.

## *DISCUSSION*

After everyone is finished with the Bible study, ask group members for their answers. Pause after each verse to discuss the questions listed below. List the qualities on the chalkboard or an overhead transparency as they are given, and have group members complete their Workout Sheets if they did not look up all the references.

- **Proverbs 17:17a** (A friend loves at all times, even when he or she does not agree with you.) **What are some times when friends may not agree with each other?**
- **Proverbs 18:24** (A friend sticks closer than a brother.) **In what ways is a good friend closer than a brother or sister?**
- **Proverbs 27:17** (A friend sharpens our disposition, character, skills, etc.) **How do friends keep us sharp?**
- **Proverbs 27:6** (A friend tells the truth even when it hurts.) **What are some examples of the truth hurting us?**
- **Proverbs 27:9** (A friend gives counsel, advice.) **What kinds of advice do friends give that help us? That do not help?**
- **Proverbs 11:13** (A friend does not tell secrets.) **Can you think of a time when a friend told your secret to someone else? How did you feel?**
- **John 15:13** (A friend loves even to the point of dying for someone else.) **How can friends show love for one another?**
- **Romans 14:19** (A friend builds me up.) **How can friends build up one another?**
- **Romans 15:7** (A friend accepts me, including my faults.) **How can friends show that they accept each other?**

- **Philippians 2:3-4** (A friend puts others before his own selfish interests.) **How can friends put others before themselves?**

Discuss how these qualities of a friend compare with the ones illustrated on the montages.

# APPLYING THE TRUTH

### *WORKOUT SHEET*

Distribute copies of Workout Sheet #6, "Need a Friend? Be a Friend!" Referring to the list on the board or overhead, to the montages, to chapter 3 in the student book, and to the friendship symbols if you did that activity, have everyone list the five qualities they think are most important in a friend.



Then have them rate themselves on these qualities, asking them to determine how well they are being a friend to others in these areas. Have them draw a smiling face in the circle if they have that quality, a sad face if they do not, and a straight-mouthed face if they are not sure.

Instruct each group member to choose one quality with a sad or straight-mouthed face, put a check after the quality, and list on the bottom half several steps he can take this week to be a better friend in that area.

If necessary, discuss specific ways to cultivate several sample qualities. For instance:

- Keeps secrets—apologize to the person whose secret you told; determine not to tell a secret; ask God to help you keep your mouth closed.
- Thoughtful—plan a surprise for a friend; let your friend choose the next activity; buy a friendship card and send it; offer to help a friend do a chore.

### *SONG (Optional)*

Play the song "Friends." Ask group members to decide silently if their friends could say the same things about them.

### *PRAYER*

Close with a few minutes of silent prayer, encouraging everyone to ask God to help him be a better friend by following through on the steps for improvement which he wrote down.

Let group members take home the montages if they want to. If more than one person in a group wants it, cut it into sections or draw a name.

WORKOUT SHEET # 5

Find out what God's Word has to say about quality friendship. Complete the following statements based on the Bible verses listed.

**PROVERBS 17:17a**

A friend ______________________________
______________________________
______________________________
______________________________
______________________________.

**PROVERBS 18:24**

A friend ______________________________
______________________________
______________________________
______________________________
______________________________.

**PROVERBS 27:17**

A friend ______________________________
______________________________
______________________________
______________________________
______________________________.

**PROVERBS 27:6**

A friend ______________________________
______________________________
______________________________
______________________________
______________________________.

**PROVERBS 27:9**

A friend ______________________________
______________________________
______________________________
______________________________
______________________________.

**PROVERBS 11:13**

A friend ______________________________
______________________________
______________________________
______________________________
______________________________.

**JOHN 15:13**

A friend ______________________________
______________________________
______________________________
______________________________
______________________________.

**ROMANS 14:19**

A friend ______________________________
______________________________
______________________________
______________________________
______________________________.

**ROMANS 15:7**

A friend ______________________________
______________________________
______________________________
______________________________
______________________________.

**PHILIPPIANS 2:3-4**

A friend ______________________________
______________________________
______________________________
______________________________
______________________________.

WORKOUT SHEET # 6

# N E E D A F R I E N D ?

**What I like best in a friend:**

○ ________________________________

○ ________________________________

○ ________________________________

○ ________________________________

○ ________________________________

**How I can be a better friend:**

1.

2.

3.

# B E A F R I E N D !

SESSION 4

# MEASURING UP ON THE FRIENDSHIP SCALE

**KEY CONCEPT**

Paul's description of love in 1 Corinthians 13 also depicts a true friend.

**MEETING THE NEED**

This session will respond to the following student questions and comments:
- "What do I do when a friend gets mad at me?"
- "I think the best thing friends can do for each other is to be kind."

**SESSION GOALS**

You will help each group member
1. explore the need for measuring standards,
2. discover God's standards for a true friend,
3. evaluate how well he measures up to God's standards for a friend.

**SPECIAL PREPARATION**

____ If you use Workout Sheet #7, mark a different item on each sheet with a yellow highlighting pen. If your group is less than 20, choose the items which you think will be most interesting to them. If your group is larger than 20, let them work in pairs or teams on an item.
____ Gather a number of measuring devices, including a cloth tape measure. See "Launching the Lesson" for examples.
____ Make at least two tape measures out of ½" strips of vinyl or heavy cloth. Using a different length for the inch on each one, mark off inches with a black marking pen.
____ Two or four sheets of poster board and boxes with construction paper, marking pens, scissors, and rubber cement

# BUILDING THE BODY

Use one, two, or all of the following activities to get your session off to an active start.

## WORKOUT SHEET

As soon as a few group members arrive, begin distributing Workout Sheet #7, "Measuring Our Group," and pencils. Instruct them to talk to everyone to find out the total for their highlighted item.

When time is up, quickly go over the items to find the totals. Mention that these items are only a few of many ways to measure a group.

## BLIND MEASURE UP

Divide your group into at least two teams with a maximum of eight to ten on a team. Have each team stand in a clear area large enough to move around without bumping into furniture or walls. Appoint one person from each team to act as spotter to be certain that no one gets hurt.

Tell everyone to close their eyes before you give directions. They are to keep their eyes and mouths closed at all times—no peeking and no talking. Tell each team to line up according to height; let the team members decide which end will be the shortest. The team which finishes fastest with the most number of people in correct order is the winner. Try the game again but have teams line up by shoe size or arm length.

When finished, take a few minutes to discuss briefly the following questions:

- **How did each team decide which end would be the shortest?**
- **How did you feel during this game?**
- **What are some standards that other people set which you are expected to measure up to?** (For example, teachers set grade scales, peers decide what are acceptable clothes to wear and things to do, parents make rules which children are to obey, piano teachers tell how many hours to practice each week.)

## COMPARISON SCAVENGER HUNT

Divide your group into two or more teams. Give each team a pencil and list of the following items to find around the church building. (Adapt the list for other meeting places or for items which group members have with them.) Instruct teams to write down where they found things that need to be returned. You may want to set a time limit for searching. The team with the most winning items is the overall winner.

1. Oldest penny
2. Smelliest sock
3. Largest book

4. Most worn-out shoe
5. Smallest Bible (New Testament doesn't count)
6. Longest pencil
7. Oldest-dated Sunday school take-home paper
8. Smallest toy
9. Newest looking hymnbook
10. Oldest church bulletin
11. Photograph with the most people
12. Smallest blue object
13. Largest red object
14. Shortest shoe
15. Biggest piece of paper
16. Longest piece of chalk
17. Newest chalk eraser
18. Most combs
19. Newest crayon
20. Most shoe strings



# LAUNCHING THE LESSON

### *MEASURING DEVICES DISPLAY*

Bring a number of measuring devices, such as bathroom scales, tape measure, yardstick, measuring cup, measuring spoons, diet scale, clock, stopwatch, and kitchen timer. Display the items, perhaps demonstrating a few like the bathroom scales and the stopwatch. Ask what they all have in common.

Then measure a volunteer's waist with your homemade and official tape measures, announcing the different sizes. Ham it up as you do so. Ask why standard measurements are important.

Say something like: **Just as standard measurements help us function in the physical world, so biblical standards help us function in relationships.**

# EXPLORING THE WORD

### *PARAPHRASE*

Have everyone turn to 1 Corinthians 13. Introduce this chapter as Paul's description of how love acts. Point out that we can substitute the words *a friend* for love, especially in verses 4-8a, and we have an excellent standard for measuring how good a friend we are.

Read verses 4-8a together, replacing the word *love* with *a friend*. Read it like that a second time, asking group members to think about what they are reading.

### POSTERS

Introduce the next activity by saying something like: **Let's explore ways friends can practice these verses.** Divide group members into two or four groups, depending on the number, and appoint leaders. Call one group the positives and the other, the negatives. If you have four groups, assign two to each category. Give each group a sheet of poster board and a box of supplies. Instruct them to label their poster "A friend is" or "A friend is not." Then they should illustrate with pictures and/or words all the descriptions from 1 Corinthians 13:4-8a which fit the category. For example, show a teen helping someone with kindness. The negative group could draw pictures of the wrong actions and mark an "X" over them.

Make sure everyone understands that the negatives look for statements with the words *not, no, never* and vice versa. Refer group members to the chapter in the student book for definitions, or provide dictionaries for looking up unfamiliar words.

The positives group should include illustrations of the following characteristics of a friend: patience, kindness, rejoicing with the truth, protection, trust, hope, perseverance.

The negatives group should include illustrations of these characteristics of a friend: no envy, no boasting, no pride, no rudeness, no self-seeking, no quick anger, no keeping record of wrongs, no delight in evil, no failing.

Allow the groups about 20-30 minutes to complete their posters. Then have a representative from each group show and briefly explain their poster. As you have time, discuss other ways to demonstrate each characteristic.

## APPLYING THE TRUTH

### WORKOUT SHEET

Ask everyone to think about how he measures up to this standard for friends in 1 Corinthians 13. Distribute Workout Sheet #8, "Measuring Up." Instruct each group member to look at the passage again, and write the characteristics which are presently true of himself next to the marks on the yardstick.

Then have everyone choose a description he needs to work on in order to be a better friend, and fill in the bottom of the sheet.

### PRAYER

Have group members pair off, share what they wrote on the bottom of the Workout Sheet, and pray specifically for each other.

# MEASURING OUR

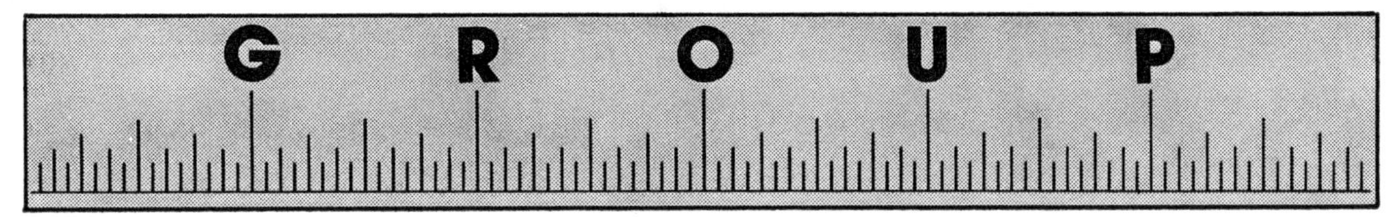


***Talk to your fellow group members to find out the total number for the item below which is highlighted in yellow.***

*TOTAL*

___ **S**tates/countries born in

___ **M**usical instruments have had experience on

___ **P**ets

___ **Y**ears attended church regularly

___ **B**rothers and sisters

___ **E**ighth graders

___ **M**embers of a school sports team

___ **F**eet in height

___ **S**eventh graders

___ **F**irstborn child in the family

___ **B**'s on the last report card

___ **B**ooks read in the last week that were not for a school assignment

___ **R**oller coaster riders

___ **B**roccoli eaters

___ **S**tuffed animals owned

___ **L**eft-handers

___ **R**adios owned

___ **B**irthdays this month

___ **T**onsils not removed

___ **B**roken bones

WORKOUT SHEET # 8

**N**ext to the marks on the yardstick below, write the words or phrases from 1 Corinthians 13:4-8a which describe you as a friend.

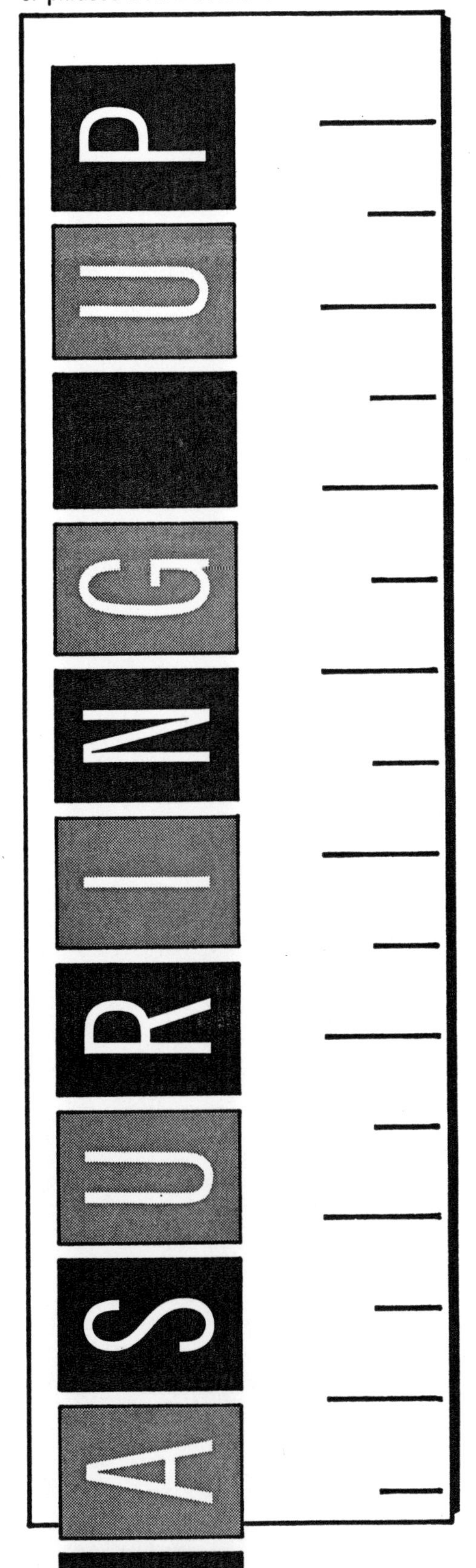


**C**hoose one description of a friend that you need to work on:

______________________________________________

**L**ist two or three specific steps you will take this week to begin to measure up to that description:

______________________________________________

______________________________________________

______________________________________________

# PART TWO

## ...HOW DO THEY ACT?

Learning how to make friends is a skill most young teens need to work at to develop. They want to have lots of friends, but many do not know how to reach out and make them. Instead, they stand back, waiting for someone else to make the first move. In this second section on friendship, you can help your group members develop skills which will last a lifetime.

Since friendships begin with conversations, the first session focuses on how to start them. Even though most young teens do a lot of talking, they tend to be hesitant with people they don't know very well or not at all. During this session, your group members will learn how to ask questions in order to begin conversations and then practice with each other to feel more comfortable doing so.

An important part of good conversation is knowing how to listen. So during Session 6 you will teach your group members listening skills and again have them practice with each other.

Once they know how to talk and listen, young teens are better equipped to reach out to others to begin friendships instead of waiting for others to make the first move. In Session 7 they will study how Barnabas reached out to Paul and how to overcome three attitudes which often prevent us from following his example.

Finally, you will complete this section by building on the previous three sessions to challenge your group members to show their faith in Christ and teach them how to share their faith verbally.

# FRIENDS—HOW DO THEY ACT?

## SESSION 5

# *SPEAKING OF FRIENDSHIP*

**KEY CONCEPT**

A key to making new friends is knowing questions to ask.

**MEETING THE NEED**

This session will respond to the following student comments:

- "The biggest difficulty I have in making friends is going up to them and talking."
- "I don't know what to say to people I don't know."
- "The hardest thing about making friends is either I'm shy or else they are shy."

**SESSION GOALS**

You will help each group member

1. observe conversation problems,
2. analyze some of Jesus' conversations, and become acquainted with ways to start conversations,
3. practice starting conversations.

**SPECIAL PREPARATION**

____ Prepare half sheets of paper for "Interest Match," one for each group member.

____ Ask group members to act out the opening conversation from the student book. Or have two people record the conversation in "Dialogue."

____ Complete Workout Sheet #10 before looking at the answers to be sure you understand this activity.

____ Prepare the poster or overhead transparency for the talk-to in "Exploring the Word." Cover each point with paper which can be easily removed to reveal one point at a time.

____ Practice the talk-to so you can deliver it without reading the information.

____ Write several questions for group members to reword for point #3 in the lecture.

# BUILDING THE BODY

Start your session in a more active way by using one or both of these activities.

### WORKOUT SHEET

Distribute Workout Sheet #9, "May I Have Your Autograph?" and pencils. Have everyone collect the signatures of people who match the descriptions on the sheet.

### INTEREST MATCH

Distribute half sheets of paper and pencils. Instruct everyone to write down five things they most like to do or are interested in, such as sleeping late, reading, playing football, singing. After everyone has completed his list, tell them to find five other people who each share one of those interests (they don't have to be listed on their own sheets) and ask them to sign their names next to the common interest. No one can sign more than once on a sheet.



# LAUNCHING THE LESSON

### STUDENT BOOK OPTION

Have the two preselected teens act out the opening conversation from the student book. When they finish, ask "Bob" how he felt when "Phil" talked in monosyllables. Then ask for feedback from the rest of the group. **What are your reactions to this conversation?**

Say something like: **It's conversations like this one that make us want to give up trying to get to know other people. But there are some guidelines we can follow to prevent this from happening.**

### DIALOGUE

If you aren't using the student books, have two people record the following conversation. Change the names if necessary. The person who plays Phil should speak with very little expression. Play the tape to begin the lesson.

BOB: **Hi, Phil. How's it going?**

PHIL: **OK.**

BOB: **Did you get the book read for English?**

PHIL: **Yes.**

BOB: **Did you like it?**

PHIL: **No.**

BOB: **Are you going to the basketball tryouts?**

PHIL: **Maybe.**

BOB: **You should. I've seen you play, and you're pretty good.**

PHIL: **I guess.**

BOB: **Are you going to the game this weekend?**

PHIL: **Probably.**

BOB: **Good. Well, I've got to go. See you around.**

Use the discussion question and transition from "Student Book Option."



# EXPLORING THE WORD

## *WORKOUT SHEET*

Introduce the next step in the session: **For the next few minutes, you are going to be detectives. Your first assignment is to analyze some of Jesus' conversations for clues to talking with people.** Distribute Workout Sheet #10, "Conversation Clues," and pencils. Go over the directions and do John 8:9-11 together to be sure everyone understands the assignment. Write your analysis on the chalkboard or an overhead transparency. It should look like this (explanations are in parentheses):

J—?s (Jesus asked two questions)
W—A (woman answered)
J—R (Jesus responded to her answer)

Divide group members into two or four groups, depending on the number present. Assign John 1:35-39 and 4:5-26 to one or two groups and Luke 24:13-27 and John 3:1-16 to the other group(s) to analyze.

Call for reports. Write the analyses on the board or transparency. They should be similar to the ones below.

John 1:35-39
J—?
D—?
J—A

John 4:5-26
J—?
S—S, ?
J—A
S—R, ?s
J—A
S—R
J—S
S—R
J—R
S—R
J—R
S—R
J—R

Luke 24:13-27
J—?
D—?
J—?

John 3:1-16
N—S
J—R
N—?, S

D—A
J—R

J—R
N—?
J—?, Ss

Discuss: **What did you learn about conversations from this study?** If group members didn't notice, point out the frequency of questions.

## TALK-TO

Display your poster or overhead transparency with the following information in italics. Reveal each point as you talk about it.

Say something like: **Here are seven suggestions on how to take the mystery out of starting conversations.**

***1. Introduce yourself.*** **If you don't know the person, say, "Hi, my name is ______." If the other person doesn't respond, ask for his or her name.**

***2. Express interest.*** **Make an appropriate comment or ask a question. For example, if she is holding a book, ask, "How do you like that book?" If you're at school, ask, "What classes are you taking?" or "Who do you have for English?" Or tell the person you like his shirt, etc.**

***3. Ask good questions.*** **Don't ask questions that can be answered with a "yes" or "no." They kill a conversation instead of carrying it along. Instead, ask questions that begin with the words *who, what, when, where, why,* and *how.***

Ask group members for examples of each type of question. For instance:

- Who are your favorite musicians?
- What do you like to do in your free time?
- When do you plan to go to the game?
- Where do you like to go on vacation?
- Why do you like to go there?
- How do you like this study on friends?

If you are using the student books, have everyone look at the opening conversation in chapter 5. Ask them to reword Bob's questions to avoid getting yes or no answers. Examples are given below.

- Did you get the book read for English? (How much of the book for English have you read?)
- Did you like it? (How did you like it? What did you like best about it?)
- Are you going to the basketball tryouts? (Who do you think will try out for the basketball team?)
- Are you going to the game this weekend? (What do you plan to do this weekend?)

If you aren't using the student books, give your group members several questions with yes or no answers, and ask them to reword each. For example, "Are you in Mrs. W's history class?" should be "Whose history class are you in?"

**4. *Build on what the other person tells you, and ask follow-up questions.* If he volunteers information beyond answering your question, he probably wants to talk about that. For example, you ask who his history teacher is. He tells you and also mentions that he doesn't like her. That's a clue to ask, "Why don't you like her?" Even if he doesn't give you extra information, you can ask a follow-up question, such as, "How do you like her?" or "Will you tell me more?"**

**5. *Listen.* Concentrate on what the other person is telling you, not on what you will say next.**

**6. *Tell about yourself.* Don't just interview the other person by asking question after question. Share information about yourself which is related to the questions you are asking.**

**7. *Silences are OK.* Don't be afraid of pauses in the conversation. We all need time to think in order to respond to questions or to change topics. Besides, most people do not talk nonstop.**

Answer any questions your group members may have about any of these guidelines.



# APPLYING THE TRUTH

## CONVERSATION PRACTICE

Instruct everyone to pair off with someone they don't know very well and begin a conversation. After about 5 minutes, reassemble the group.

## DISCUSSION

Discuss the following questions:

- **What was good about your conversation?**
- **What problems did you encounter?**
- **What did you learn about the other person?**

## ASSIGNMENT

Encourage everyone to start at least one conversation a day with someone at school they don't know.

## PRAYER

Have a few minutes of sentence prayers, encouraging each group member to ask for God's help in becoming better at starting conversations with young teens and others they don't know.

Collect the signatures of people who match these descriptions.
A person may not sign more than one square on your sheet. You cannot sign your own.

| | | | |
|---|---|---|---|
| Has a pet. ■ | Can play a musical instrument. ■ | Has the last birthday of the year. ■ | Has lived in more than one state. ■ |
| Lives in an apartment. ■ | Uses the same brand of tooth-paste you do. ■ | Can sing. ■ | Likes to draw. ■ |
| Weighs less than 100 pounds. ■ | Dislikes science classes. ■ | Has been a Christian for less than three years. ■ | Wears a size-6 shoe. ■ |
| Lives the farthest from you. ■ | Owns a bike. ■ | Has the first birthday of the year. ■ | Has attended a camp for at least a week. ■ |

# CONVERSATION CLUES

As Detective for a Day, your assignment is to check out Jesus' conversations. You'll find some of them in the following Bible passages. Look them up and analyze the conversation. Indicate who spoke by using that person's first initial; then tell how he or she spoke, using these symbols:

*question* = **?**
*answer* = **A**
*statement* = **S**
*response to an answer*
*or other statement* = **R**

**John 8:9-11**

**John 1:35-39**

**John 3:1-16**

**Luke 24:13-27**

**John 4:5-26**

# FRIENDS — HOW DO THEY ACT?

*SESSION 6*

## *IS ANYBODY OUT THERE LISTENING?*

**KEY CONCEPT**

Friends learn to listen to others.

**MEETING THE NEED**

This session will respond to the following student comments:
- "Sometimes we don't understand each other's point of view."
- "I wish my friends would listen better."

**SESSION GOALS**

You will help each group member
1. experience listening difficulties,
2. identify guidelines for effective listening,
3. practice listening skills.

**SPECIAL PREPARATION**

____ Borrow a sound effects record and bring a record player, or collect items for making a variety of sounds for "Listening Test."
____ Half sheets of paper for "Listening Test," one for each group member
____ Write the names of animals on slips of paper and fold them in half for "Barnyard."
____ Choose phrases for the gossip game in "Launching the Lesson."

# BUILDING THE BODY

Use one or both of the following activities to help your group members begin to think about how important listening is.

### LISTENING TEST

Borrow a sound effects record from your local library, or bring items needed to make different sounds. Give each group member a half sheet of paper and a pencil. Tell everyone to number from 1 to 15 on the paper. As you play (or make without being seen) each sound, have everyone write down what it is. Start with a few easy sounds and get progressively harder. Be certain at least a few will take careful listening to identify. Keep the pace lively, and don't repeat any.

After you have played all the sounds, identify them while everyone grades his or her own paper. Discuss how important careful listening was in order to identify the sounds.



### LISTENING ROUNDUP

Write the names of several animals on slips of paper, making sure you have at least two or three of each. Some suggestions are: cat, dog, cow, pig, horse, donkey, chicken. Fold the slips in half, and mix them up so you don't give the same animal to teens who are standing together. Have group members stand in the middle of the room. Pass out the slips of paper, cautioning everyone to keep his animal a secret. Tell the group that on your signal they are to close their eyes and make the sound of their animals, in order to form a group with everyone else who is making the same sound. No other talking or signaling is allowed. Continue until all animal units have formed.

Ask group members how they were able to find the people who were the same animal as themselves. Discuss how important listening was to completing the task.

# LAUNCHING THE LESSON

### GOSSIP GAME

Play a round or two of the game of gossip. Have group members stand or sit in straight lines with about ten per line. Tell them you want to test their listening skills. Whisper a statement about listening to the first person; i.e., "If you want to be a good friend, you need to learn how to listen." Have that person whisper what he heard to the next person, etc. No repeats are allowed. The last person tells what he heard aloud.

Point out that listening is more than just hearing the words the other person is saying.

### STUDENT BOOK OPTION

Have three volunteers read or act out the situations with Kelly at the beginning of the chapter in the student book. Ask group members to identify similar situations in their own lives and how they felt when the other person wasn't listening.

Say something like: **Let's look at what God says about listening, and then we'll practice several listening skills.**

# EXPLORING THE WORD

### BIBLE SEARCH AND LIST

One at a time, have everyone look up the following verses to discover what they say about listening. Use the accompanying questions to guide your discussion. After talking about each verse, list guidelines for effective listening on the chalkboard or an overhead transparency.

- **Proverbs 4:20. How do you know if someone is paying attention to you when you're talking?** (He looks at you, he looks interested, he doesn't interrupt.)

- **Proverbs 18:13. How does a person answer before listening?** (He interrupts to say what he thinks before knowing all the facts.)

- **James 1:19. How can we be "quick to listen, slow to speak"?** (Let the other person talk without interrupting, don't argue or criticize while he's talking, don't start talking about yourself.)

- **Isaiah 42:20b. What does listening but not hearing mean? What keeps us from really hearing someone else?** (Thinking about something else or what you're going to say next, not listening with the heart [being aware of the other person's feelings].)

Your listening guidelines should include the following:

- Look at the person talking.
- Be genuinely interested.
- Don't interrupt.
- Don't argue or criticize.
- Think about what the other person is saying.
- Listen for feelings.

Ask group members to add any other guidelines they can think of.

### DEMONSTRATION

Say: **Part of listening is paying attention to body language.** Demonstrate what body language says by folding your arms, sitting on the edge of your chair, swinging your leg nervously, clenching your fist, etc. Ask group members to tell what they see.

Ask for volunteers who can demonstrate various types of body language. Give them an attitude to act out, such as "I'm shy," "I'm bored," "I'm irritated," etc. You might want to assign the attitude secretly so class members can guess what is being portrayed.

## WORKOUT SHEET

**Another example of reading body language is discerning how a person is feeling by his facial expression.**

Distribute Workout Sheet #11, "Name That Feeling," and pencils. Instruct group members to study each face on the sheet and write down what they think that person is feeling. When everyone is finished, ask for responses. Correct answers are: (1) happiness, (2) sadness, (3) disgust, (4) fear, (5) anger, and (6) surprise.



Add another guideline to your listening list:

- Study the other person's body language.

## LISTENING PRACTICE

Pair off group members, splitting up best friends and keeping the same sex together. Announce that the one with the next birthday will be the talker and the other person will be the listener. Tell group members that on your signal the talkers are to tell their partners about what happened at school this week. The listeners are to break as many of the guidelines on your list as they can. After 2-3 minutes, have the partners switch roles and repeat this exercise.

Repeat the exercise again with the listeners following the guidelines. Give each person an opportunity to be a listener.

Ask: **How did you feel when your partner didn't listen to you? How did you feel when he or she did listen?**

## DEMONSTRATION

Explain that there's another guideline for good listening:

- Clarify to be sure you understand.

Add it to your list. **We may think we know what the other person means but not really understand at all. So we need to ask questions and to paraphrase to be sure we understand.**

Demonstrate this guideline by asking for a volunteer to talk with you about a bad experience that happened recently. Sit with the volunteer where everyone can observe you, and converse for a couple of minutes. As you listen to what he or she says, clarify with appropriate statements ("You must have felt angry"), ask questions ("Do you mean that . . ."), and paraphrase ("You mean that you . . .").

### LISTENING PRACTICE

Instruct group members to get together with their partners again. (Or you may want to form new pairs.) Have the original talkers take that role again and tell their partners about the best thing that happened to them recently. The listeners should practice asking questions and clarifying what they hear. After a couple of minutes, have everyone switch roles and repeat the exercise.

Discuss: **How did you feel when you were talking and the other person really tried to understand what you were saying? How did you feel when you were listening and trying to clarify what the other person was saying?** Most of your group members probably felt awkward during this practice, but point out that these skills become more natural with use.



## APPLYING THE TRUTH

### WORKOUT SHEET

Distribute Workout Sheet #12, "Are You Listening?" Have everyone rate themselves as listeners. If you listed other guidelines during the study, have group members write them in the blank boxes. Then instruct them to choose a skill they need to work on most and practice it this week.

### PRAYER

Close with prayer, thanking God that He is a good listener and asking for His help to develop the listening skills you have just practiced.

# NAME THAT FEELING

*Study the six faces below. What is each person feeling? Write your guess on the line below each picture.*

1. ..................

2. ..................

3. ..................

4. ..................

5. ..................

6. ..................

# ARE YOU LISTENING?

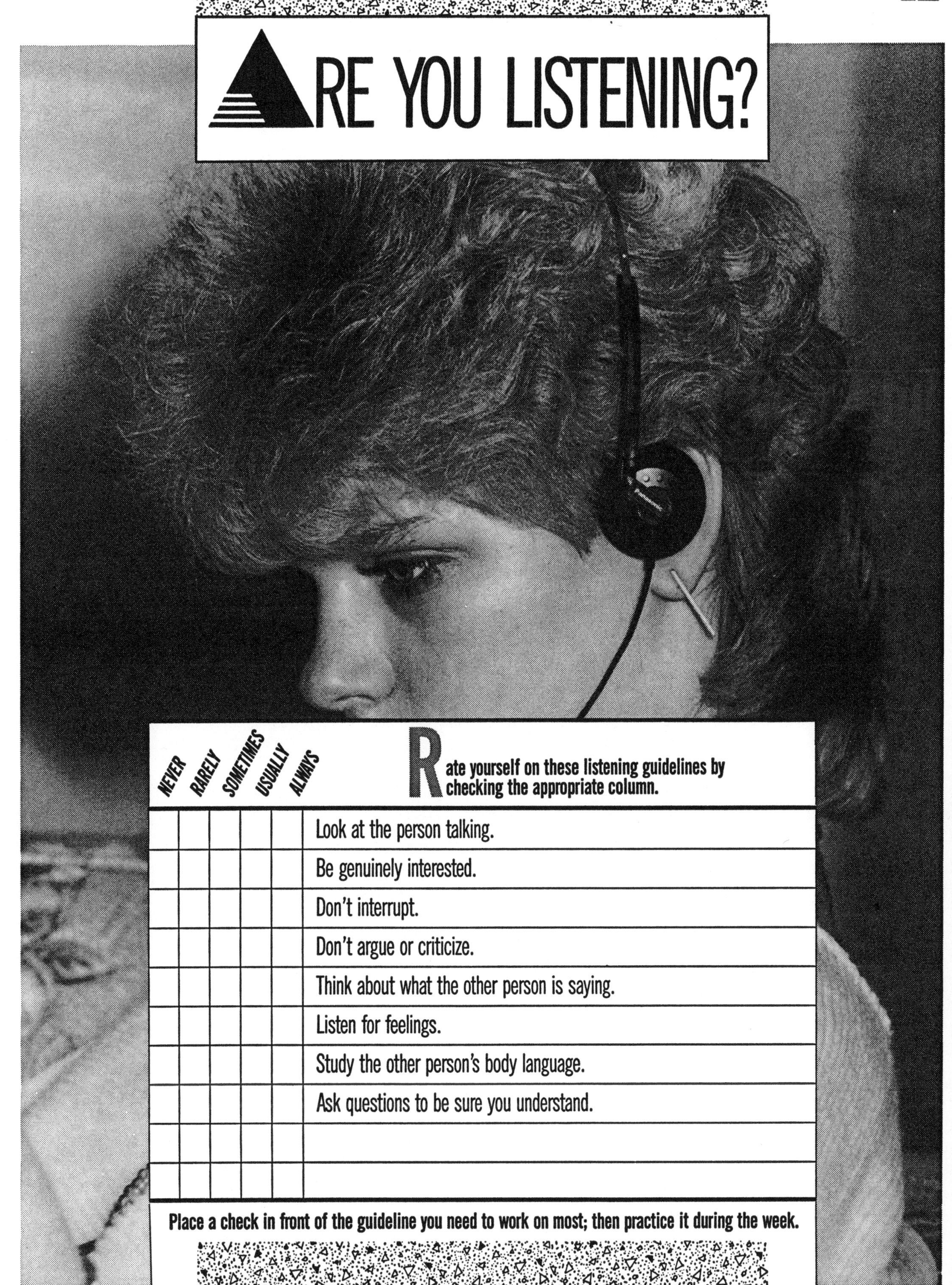

**Rate yourself on these listening guidelines by checking the appropriate column.**

| NEVER | RARELY | SOMETIMES | USUALLY | ALWAYS | |
|---|---|---|---|---|---|
| | | | | | Look at the person talking. |
| | | | | | Be genuinely interested. |
| | | | | | Don't interrupt. |
| | | | | | Don't argue or criticize. |
| | | | | | Think about what the other person is saying. |
| | | | | | Listen for feelings. |
| | | | | | Study the other person's body language. |
| | | | | | Ask questions to be sure you understand. |
| | | | | | |
| | | | | | |

**Place a check in front of the guideline you need to work on most; then practice it during the week.**

# FRIENDS—HOW DO THEY ACT?

*SESSION 7*

## *A FRIEND IN DEED*

**KEY CONCEPT**

To have friends we must reach out to others.

**MEETING THE NEED**

This session will respond to the following student comments:
- "I wish I had more friends."
- "It's too hard to make new friends."

**SESSION GOALS**

You will help each group member
1. interpret a relationship situation,
2. discover how Barnabas reached out to Saul, and how to overcome attitudes that prevent reaching out,
3. choose one thing to do each day this week to reach out to make new friends.

**SPECIAL PREPARATION**

____ Draw three large rocks on an overhead transparency. Label each one with an attitude and the accompanying two Bible references as given in "Exploring the Word." Or make the rocks out of construction paper and bring masking tape.

# BUILDING THE BODY

Use one or both of the following games to get this session off to an active start and to help your group members begin thinking about the topic of reaching out to others.

### REACH OUT AND TOUCH

Have group members stand in one or more circles with a maximum of ten people in each. Instruct everyone to put their right hands into the circle and grab someone else's hand who is at least two people away from him. Repeat the process with the left hands but with different people. Then tell them to untangle without letting go.

When the circles have untangled, briefly discuss how group members felt when you told them to untangle. Most will say it seemed to be an impossible task. Ask them how they felt when they finished. Compare the change in feelings to what we go through when reaching out to become friends with someone new.

### HUMAN TWISTER

Have group members stand in the center of the room. Explain that you will call out body parts, and everyone must quickly match that part to the corresponding part of someone else. For example, if you call out hand to knee, one person will put his hand on another person's knee. You can also call out the same parts, i.e., nose to nose. Start out slowly, then gradually speed up.

Take a few minutes at the end of the game to talk about how some group members reached out quickly and others waited for someone to come up to them. Mention that the same situation exists in forming friendships.

# LAUNCHING THE LESSON

### WORKOUT SHEET

Distribute Workout Sheet #13, "Cartoonist for a Day," and pencils. Have group members look at the cartoon frames and complete the story by filling in what the guy in frame 3 is thinking and then drawing the conclusion in frame 4.

When everyone is finished, ask volunteers to share their stories. Talk about the diversity or sameness in their stories and compare them to how people do or do not reach out to others to make friends. Then introduce Barnabas as an example of how to take the first step to have more friends.

# EXPLORING THE WORD

## BIBLE STUDY

Have everyone turn to Acts 9. Ask two volunteers to read verses 1-8 and 20-28 aloud. Use the following questions to help group members discover how Barnabas was a friend who reached out to Saul (Paul).

- **What kind of person was Saul?** (He hated Christians, threatening them and obtaining permission to imprison them.)
- **What happened to Saul on his way to Damascus to get Christian prisoners?** (He met Jesus and became a believer.)
- **What did Saul do after he became a Christian?** (He preached that Jesus is God's Son in the Jewish synagogues.)
- **How did the Jewish people react?** (They were astonished that Saul preached Jesus and didn't believe he was the same man who had persecuted Christians. They also plotted to kill him.)
- **Paul escaped from those trying to kill him and went to Jerusalem. What did he do when he got there?** (He tried to join the Christians.)
- **How did the Christians react to him?** (They were afraid Saul was trying to trick them and didn't believe he was really a Christian.)
- **How did Barnabas react?** (He brought Saul to the church leaders and explained how he became a Christian.)
- **How was Barnabas a good friend?** (He reached out to someone who was new and needed a friend.)
- **Do you think Saul would have been Barnabas' friend if Barnabas had not reached out first? Why or why not?** (Group members may be divided on this question. If so, take time to hear both sides.)

  If group members have difficulty answering this question, have them imagine that they want to be friends with a certain group at school, but no one in that group will speak with them. How would they feel? [Rejected, discouraged.] What if one person in that group decided to be friends with them? How would they feel then? [Accepted, happy.]

- **How do you think Saul felt when Barnabas became his friend?**
- **What happened as a result of Barnabas' reaching out to the new person?** (Other Christians accepted Saul, and he was able to minister for the Lord without opposition from his fellow believers.)

## STUDENT BOOK OPTION

Refer to the story of David and Mephibosheth in the student book. Point out that David is another example of someone who took the first step to begin a relationship.

If you have time, you may want to look at 2 Samuel 9 together and discuss some of the above questions as they relate to David and Mephibosheth.

Ask group members if they can think of a time when someone else made the first move to become friends with them like Liz and Diane did with the author of the book. Ask how they felt before and after that person reached out to them.

## STUMBLING BLOCKS

Say something like: **Barnabas is a good example of how we often have to make the first move if we're going to make new friends. But sometimes we struggle with certain attitudes which get in the way of our reaching out to others. Let's look at three of these.**



Show your transparency with the three rocks labeled with the following attitudes and Bible references. Or tape your construction paper rocks to the chalkboard or wall. Divide your group into three sections, and assign one stumbling block to each section. Let group members work in pairs.

First have each pair discuss how the attitude is a stumbling block to making new friends. Then have them look up the Bible verses to find out what they teach that can help us overcome that stumbling block.

When everyone is finished, ask for reports. Use the following information to supplement as necessary.

- **Fear of rejection**
  This fear keeps us from reaching out to others so we don't have to face possible rejection from them. Usually the fear is unfounded, and we miss opportunities to become friends.

  Romans 8:31—No matter what we fear, God is for us—and with us. We don't need to be afraid because God is on our side, and He's greater than our fear.

  1 Peter 5:6-7—We need to tell God about our fear and ask for His help to overcome it. As a result He gives us courage to take the first step toward making friends with someone.

- **Shyness**
  People who are shy usually have great difficulty talking to strangers and therefore making friends. It's a lot more comfortable to stay with people we know than to speak to people we don't know.

  Psalm 138:3—Just as David gained boldness from God after he prayed, we can too.

  2 Corinthians 12:9—God likes to work through our weaknesses to show us and others how powerful He is. Consequently, as we depend on Him to help us talk to new people, He can work through us to help us get past our shyness.

- **Judgmental attitude**
  When we label people and judge them as inferior to us so we feel superior, we put up walls between us and them, keeping us separated instead of reaching out to be friends.

  Philippians 2:3—If we put other people before ourselves, we make them feel important. Consequently, they like being with us because we're not stuck up.

  Colossians 3:12-13—The opposite of judging others is being kind, humble, and forgiving, qualities which promote friendships.

# APPLYING THE TRUTH

## BRAINSTORMING

Read together Matthew 7:12. Ask: **If you were looking for a friend, how would you want to be treated? How can young teens follow Barnabas' example of reaching out to others in their schools, churches, and neighborhoods?** As group members brainstorm specific ideas, list them on the chalkboard or an overhead transparency.

Suggestions might include the following: Say "Hi," smile, introduce yourself to someone you don't know, ask someone to join you for lunch, sit with someone new in a school assembly or in Sunday School class, talk to someone on the school bus who is not your friend, volunteer to show a new student around school, invite someone to your house after school or on Saturday to do homework together or goof around, send a friendship card (better yet, make it yourself).

## WORKOUT SHEET

Distribute Workout Sheet #14, "My Contract." Have everyone decide how they will reach out to make new friends this week, and write down one thing they will do each day. If possible, have them link the action with specific people. At the end of the day, they should put a check in the last column if they fulfilled their contract for that day. Point out that they are not obligated to do only what they write down; it may be more appropriate to do something else. If so, tell them to record that action. However, deciding ahead of time to do certain things makes us more likely to follow through.

Encourage each group member to put the sheet where it will be a frequent reminder to reach out like Barnabas did with Saul.

## PRAYER

Ask several volunteers to pray that each group member will overcome any stumbling blocks to reach out to make new friends this week.

Our cartoonist was unable to finish this story so you have been appointed to help him out. Study the first two frames; then write in the cloud in frame 3 what that young teen is thinking. Finally, finish the story by drawing what he does next in frame 4. Include his conversation or thoughts.

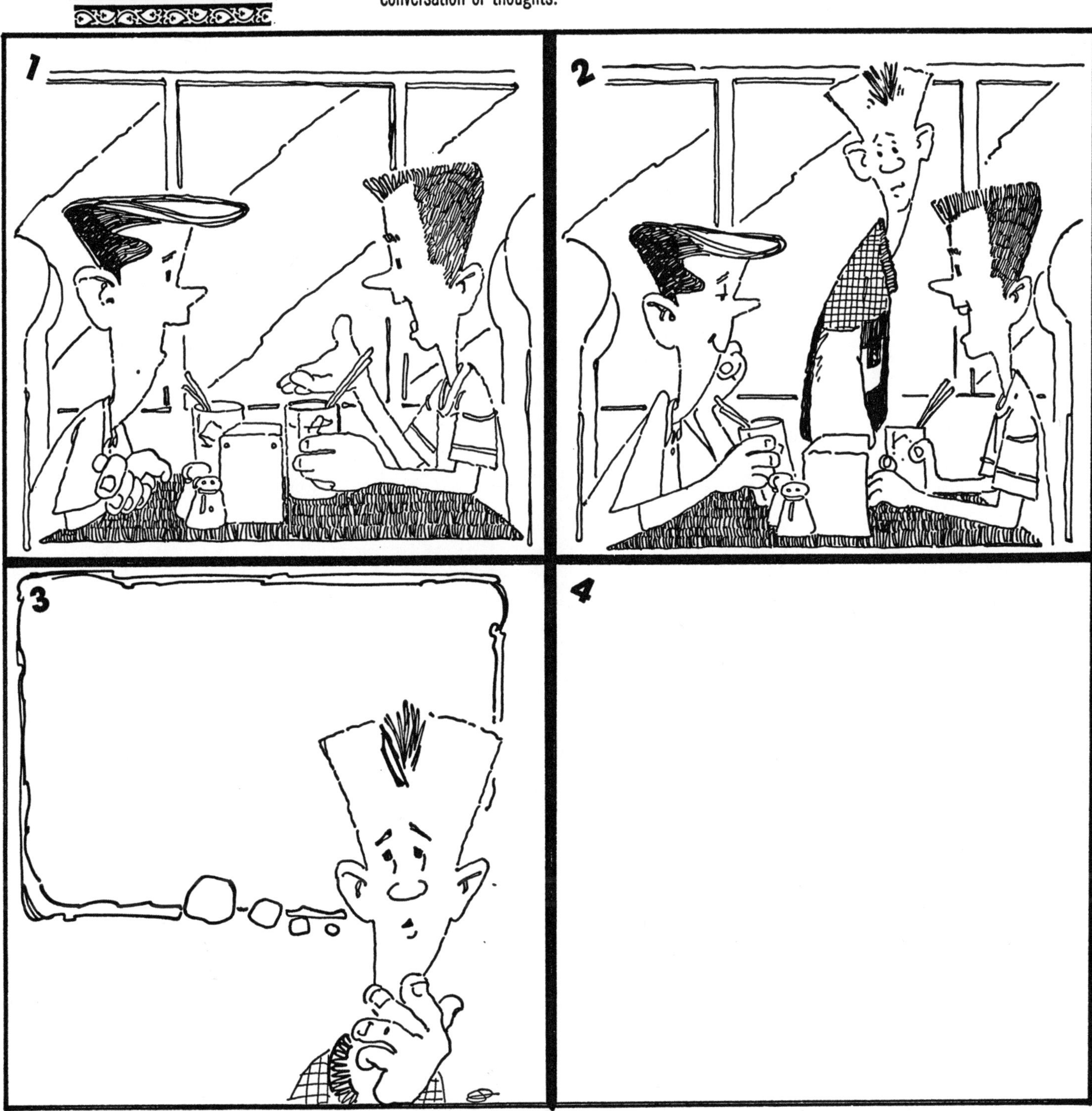

# My CONTRACT

Barnabas demonstrated the truth that to have friends, we need to be friends. Decide how you will be a friend this week by recording one thing you will do each day to make new friends. Check up on yourself daily to be sure you are keeping your contract.

| DAY | ACTION | COMPLETED |
|---|---|---|
| 1 | | |
| 2 | | |
| 3 | | |
| 4 | | |
| 5 | | |
| 6 | | |

# FRIENDS—HOW DO THEY ACT?

## *SESSION 8*

# *BUILDING BRIDGES*

**KEY CONCEPT**

Evangelism begins by sharing ourselves and our faith with non-Christian friends.

**MEETING THE NEED**

This session will respond to the following student questions and comments:
- "How can I witness to my friends without losing them?"
- "I know I should witness to my friends, but I'm afraid to."
- "If I talk to my friends about Christ, they'll think I'm weird."

**SESSION GOALS**

You will help each group member
1. develop awareness of evangelism as both showing and telling our faith,
2. explore ways to show and tell his faith,
3. choose one way to begin to share his faith with his friends.

**SPECIAL PREPARATION**

____ If possible, read *Evangelism: A Biblical Approach* by G. Michael Cocoris (Moody Press), especially chapters 8–12 and 21.

____ For "Speak and Show," draw a large oval, star, and hexagon on half sheets of poster board. Bring one sheet of paper for every two group members.

____ Write the three references from the "Bible Study" on separate sheets of paper.

____ Write the plan of salvation from "Exploring the Word" on a poster board or overhead transparency. Be sure you can explain each step. Then memorize these steps and the suggested motions for teaching them. Practice until you do not need to look at them and you feel comfortable with the motions. Bring paper to cover the steps on the plan of salvation poster or transparency.

# BUILDING THE BODY

Use one or both of these activities to get this session off to an active start.

## *ADD-ON RELAY*

Divide group members into two teams. Conduct a relay race by having the first person on each team race to a goal and back. For the second lap, the first and second persons race, holding on to each other. For the third lap, the first two people hook up with the third person. Continue until the whole team completes the last lap together. For variety, have the team members run backwards or sideways, picking up an additional person on each lap.

Compare the relay race to reaching out and inviting our friends to become part of the body of Christ through faith in Him.



## *SPEAK AND SHOW*

Draw a large oval, star, and hexagon on half sheets of poster board with a dark marking pen, one object per sheet.

Have group members count off 1, 2, 1, 2, etc. Give all the 2s a sheet of paper and a pencil. Instruct each 1 to pair up with a 2 to form a partnership. (If you have an odd number of teens, form one trio with the last 1 becoming a second 2.) Explain that one person will look at an object and describe it to their partners who will draw it.

Have the partners sit back to back with the 1s facing you. Hold up the oval, and tell the 1s to describe the object to their partners without saying what it is. The 2s will draw what their partners describe. Allow no more than 2-3 minutes. Then have the 2s compare their drawings with the oval.

Next have the partners face each other with the 2s facing you and the 1s getting the paper and pencil. Hold up the star, and instruct the 2s to describe the object only with their hands while their partners draw it. Talking and head nodding are not allowed. After 2-3 minutes, have the 1s compare their drawings with yours.

Finally, have the partners exchange paper and places so they are facing each other with the 1s facing you. Hold up the hexagon. Tell the 1s to describe the object with their hands and to answer any questions their partners ask. Volunteering information and head nodding are not allowed. Again allow 2-3 minutes, and have the 2s compare their drawings with the hexagon.

Ask group members how they felt when trying to describe an object with only words or only hand movements. How did their partners feel each time? Then discuss how the third way made it easier to draw the object. Remind group members that communication is more than words. Likewise, sharing our faith in Christ with friends involves showing as well as telling.

# LAUNCHING THE LESSON

### *COMMUNICATION GAME*

If you did not use the "Speak and Show" game from "Building the Body" to begin this session, you may want to launch the lesson with it instead of using the following activity from the student book.

### *STUDENT BOOK*

Read one or more of the case studies from the student book chapter. After each one, ask for several responses to the "why" questions.

**How we live prompts our friends to ask questions like these, and then how we answer them can lead into sharing our faith in Christ in a natural way. Let's see how we can both show and tell our faith.**



# EXPLORING THE WORD

### *BIBLE STUDY*

Have group members turn to 1 Thessalonians 2:8, and ask a volunteer to read it aloud. Ask: **What did Paul, Silas, and Timothy share with the Thessalonians when they were with them?** (The Gospel of God [verbal witness] and their lives [godly lifestyles].)

Say: **Let's look first at how we can show our faith to others.** Divide group members into three groups, appoint leaders, and give each group a sheet of paper with one of the following references. Instruct them to read the passage and list ways we can show our faith in Christ. Then tell them to think of a specific way to practice each instruction. For example, how can a young teen show hospitality to a non-Christian friend?

- **Romans 12:9-13** (Love, do what is right instead of wrong, put other people before yourself, be joyful, be patient, pray faithfully for others, help those in need, be hospitable.)

- **Romans 12:14-21** (Do good to those who do bad things to you, be sympathetic, live in harmony, don't be proud or conceited [don't act like you're better than non-Christians], don't retaliate or take revenge, do what is right, live at peace as much as possible.)

- **Ephesians 4:25-32** (Don't lie, don't hold grudges, don't steal [shoplift, cheat], don't cut people down but build them up by what you say, don't be bitter, don't lose your temper, don't talk about other people, be kind, be compassionate, forgive.)

Allow about 20 minutes; then reassemble the group. Call for reports, and list instructions from the Bible passages on the chalkboard or an overhead transparency. As you have time, ask for other examples of living out these commands. Push your teens to be specific and practical.

## WORKOUT SHEET

Say something like: **It's not enough to just live like a believer, however. We also need to verbally tell our friends about Jesus Christ. One way to do so is through sharing your testimony of how you became a Christian and how your life has changed as a result.**

Distribute Workout Sheet #15, "Telling My Story," and pencils. Instruct everyone to write out their testimonies by answering the questions on the sheet. Be alert for group members who have trouble with this activity; it may mean they are not believers even though they claim to be. Invite any who are not sure they are Christians or cannot point to any changes in their lives as a result of knowing God personally to talk with you after the session.



If possible, take time to pair off group members and have them practice telling their testimonies to each other. Doing so in this safe environment will give them more confidence to tell their friends. If you do not have time—or in addition to doing this activity—tell your group members you will call them during the week and let them practice telling you over the phone. Besides helping your young teens to build confidence, you will have an opportunity to discover if any are not Christians.

## PLAN OF SALVATION

Say: **In addition to telling our friends how we became Christians, we need to be able to explain how they can too. Let's take a few minutes to review the plan of salvation.**

Display the poster or transparency on which you have written the following six steps and Bible references. Reveal one step at a time, and ask volunteers to read the verses aloud. Explain each step, asking questions to be certain your group members understand.

1. God loves us and wants to give us eternal life (John 3:16).
2. We are separated from God because we are sinners (Romans 3:23).
3. The penalty for our sin is death (Romans 6:23a).
4. Christ paid the penalty for our sin (Romans 5:8).
5. We must trust only Christ to have eternal life (Ephesians 2:8-9).
6. Assurance (1 John 5:13).

If you have time, teach these steps with motions to help your group members remember them. Do the following motions as you repeat each step (or shortened version) and reference.

1. Loves—cross arms over your heart.
2. We—point to self; separated from God—hold arms wide apart; we—point to self; sinners—shake finger as if saying "naughty, naughty."
3. Sin—shake finger; death—choke throat with hand and look dead.
4. Christ—point to heaven; paid the penalty—make a cross with two fingers.
5. We—point to self; Christ—point to heaven.

6. Assurance—nod head yes.

Practice together and in pairs until group members can repeat all the steps and references. Encourage them to review these steps and memorize the verses since they will not always have Bibles with them when God gives them opportunities to talk to their friends.

# APPLYING THE TRUTH

## *SUMMARY*

Say something like: **Sharing our faith in Christ with our friends is a combination of showing we are different by the way we live and speak and then telling why we are different as God gives us opportunities.** Refer back to 1 Thessalonians 2:8. **Paul and his companions became acquainted with the people and shared their interests with them, one of which was their faith in Jesus Christ.**



## *WORKOUT SHEET*

Distribute Workout Sheet #16, "Be a Bridge Builder." Say: **As we try to share our faith with non-Christian friends, it helps to build some bridges to them.** Instruct group members to assess where they are in relation to their friends by writing *yes* or *no* on the bridge before each statement. Then have them complete the next section by noting the first statement with a *no* and listing several ways to correct that situation. Encourage them to include specific friends in their plans.

## *PRAYER*

If your group members are comfortable with one another, ask everyone to tell the goal he selected from the Workout Sheet and have the person on his right pray for him. Or divide the group into small groups to pray for one another. Also pray that God will help group members to show their faith and then have opportunities to tell it to their friends.

**TO HELP YOU** *be prepared to tell your friends about Jesus Christ, write out your testimony below. Practice telling it to a Christian friend; then ask God for opportunities to tell a non-Christian friend.*



# TELLING MY STORY

HOW I BECAME A CHRISTIAN:

ONE WAY MY LIFE HAS CHANGED BECAUSE I KNOW GOD PERSONALLY:

A BIBLE VERSE THAT TELLS ME I REALLY DO KNOW GOD:

# BE A BRIDGE BUILDER

Read the following statements, and write *yes* or *no* on the bridge over each statement.

***I have several non-Christian friends.***

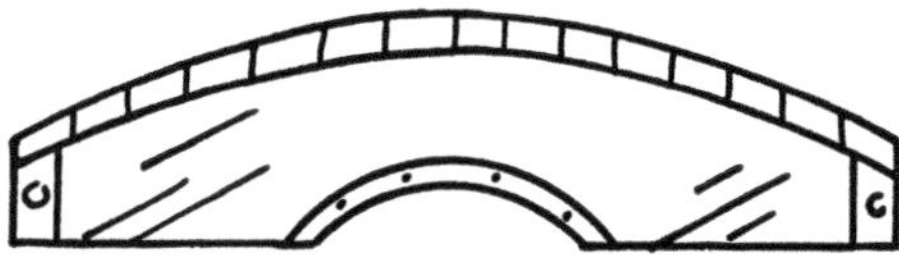

***I pray at least weekly for these friends.***

***I spend time with these friends.***

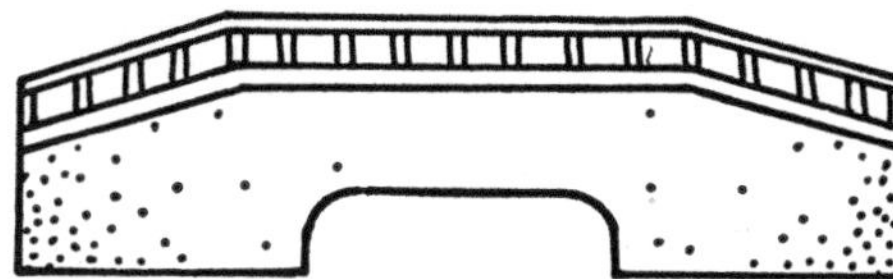

***When I am with these friends, I show my faith by the way I act and talk.***

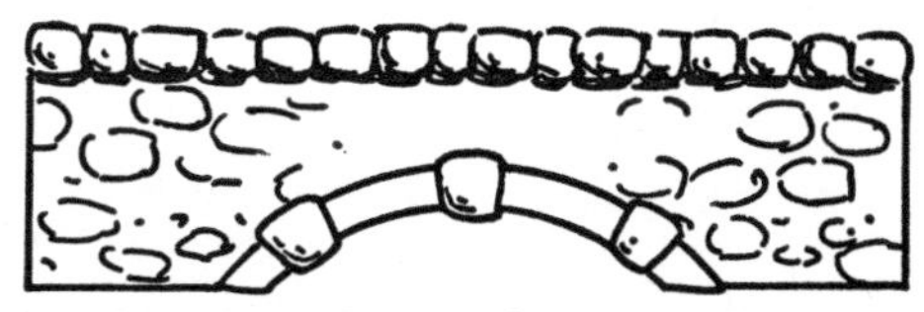

***I invite these friends to Sunday School and/or youth activities.***

***I have told my friends about my faith in Jesus Christ.***

**Choose the next bridge you need to build.**
**How will you build it?**

# PART THREE

## ...OVERCOMING OBSTACLES

Young teens are famous for their on-again, off-again friendships. One week they will be best friends with someone, and the next week those two are not speaking to each other. They are acutely aware of obstacles which get in the way of friendships, but most of them don't know how to overcome these barriers.

You will begin this last section on friendship by helping your group members gain a biblical perspective on peer pressure and popularity, two important issues for teens which often become obstacles to developing friendships with some of their peers. By investigating examples of both issues in the Bible and guidelines for dealing with them, you can encourage your young teens to stand against the negative pressures often associated with them.

In the third session of this section, you will help your group members to identify and overcome specific barriers which come between friends. And finally, in Session 12, you will teach them God's instructions for solving conflicts with their friends.

# FRIENDS— OVERCOMING OBSTACLES

## *SESSION 9*

# *SQUEEZED FROM ALL SIDES*

**KEY CONCEPT**

We don't have to give in to the pressures of friends to do wrong or to do something we don't want to do.

**MEETING THE NEED**

This session will respond to the following student questions and comments:

- "My non-Christian friends pressure me to do stuff I know is wrong. How can I tell them no without losing them as friends?"
- "My friends are always pressuring me to do what I don't want to do."
- "Some of my friends pressure me to be in style, but I can't afford the kinds of clothes they wear."

**SESSION GOALS**

You will help each group member

1. illustrate a pressure he gets from friends,
2. explore how Caleb and Joshua faced pressure, and write guidelines for dealing with pressures from friends,
3. practice using their guidelines when being pressured by friends.

**SPECIAL PREPARATION**

____ Write the words *AGREE* and *DISAGREE* on separate sheets of construction paper and bring masking tape for "Pressure Poll."

____ 2′ pieces of aluminum foil, one piece for each group member

# BUILDING THE BODY

Use one or both of the following activities to get your session off to an active start.

## *PRESSURE POLL*

Before the session begins, post the *AGREE* and *DISAGREE* signs on opposite sides of the room. Point out the signs to your group members. Tell them you are going to read a series of statements, and after each one, they are to stand by the sign which describes their answer. Use the following statements, or write ones which are more suitable for your group.

- My favorite color is blue.
- I like hot dogs better than hamburgers.
- I like Pepsi better than Coke.
- I'd rather wash dishes than dry them.
- My favorite amusement park ride is the roller coaster.
- I'd rather watch or play football than baseball.
- If I had to choose between history and science, I'd take science.
- I like to read.
- I would choose McDonald's over Burger King.
- I like school.



Discuss these questions:

- **What influenced you to choose the side you did?** (Possible responses include personal preference and not wanting to be different from the rest of the group or their close friends. Accept all answers as equally valid.)
- **When you were in the smaller group, how did you feel?** (Some young teens who are secure with their personal likes won't care which group they are in. Others will wish they were in the larger group.)
- **When you were in the larger group, how did you feel?** (At least some will probably say they were relieved to find out they like what the majority likes or that they feel more accepted or popular being in the larger group.)

## *FOLLOW THE LEADER*

If you have more than 10-12 group members, divide into two or more groups. Have each group line up, appointing the first person to be the leader. Play follow the leader, but instead of going places, have the group follow the leader's actions. Give a few suggestions, such as doing a jumping jack, turning a somersault, parting their hair on the left. Rotate leaders after a few actions so everyone has a turn.

Ask group members how they felt as leaders and then as followers. Most—if not all—of your group probably enjoyed being leaders more than followers. It's not always easy being a follower.

# LAUNCHING THE LESSON

## SCULPTURES

Give everyone about 2′ of aluminum foil, and instruct them to sculpture something that illustrates a pressure they get from their friends. For example, if someone is pressured to drink, he can make a bottle. Explain that they can mold the whole piece of foil into a shape, or tear it into a shape.

When everyone is finished, have them show and briefly explain their sculptures.

Say something like: **We all face pressures from our friends, usually to do something wrong or something we're not interested in doing. But we don't have to give in to these pressures. Let's see how we can stand against them.**



# EXPLORING THE WORD

## SKITS

Have everyone turn to Numbers 13. Explain that the nation of Israel had finished a long trek from Egypt to the land God had promised them. Now they are getting ready to enter that land.

Divide group members into three groups to study what happened. Appoint leaders, and assign one of these sections to each group: 13:16-25; 13:26-33; 14:1-10. Instruct each group to read their section and prepare to act it out for the rest of the group. Tell them they may use their Bibles for the dialogue.

After about 10-15 minutes, have each group present their skit.

## DISCUSSION

Use the following questions to discuss the events presented in the skits:

- **What peer pressure was present in this situation?** (Ten spies against two said they should not go into the Promised Land and swayed the people to their side.)
- **How do you think Joshua and Caleb felt with ten men against them?** (They probably felt pressured to give in to the majority. It would have been difficult not to agree with the rest.) **How do you think they felt with all the people against them?** (The pressure to go along with everyone else would have been enormous. Also they probably were greatly disappointed and frustrated that all these spies and people forgot God's promise to give them the land and wanted to go back to Egypt where they had been slaves under terrible circumstances.)

- **Why didn't Joshua and Caleb give in to the pressure from the other spies and then from the people?** (Cf. Numbers 14:24. They had faith in God. They knew the Lord was with them and He is greater than those against them.)

### *WORKOUT SHEET*

Say: **It's not easy to do what Joshua and Caleb did, to stand up for what you believe when a lot of people are against you. But when the pressure rises, we have the same help they had.**

Distribute Workout Sheet #17, "Pop the Pressure," and pencils. As a group look up the verses and summarize guidelines for dealing with pressures from friends to do something you don't want to do or to do something wrong. Write group members' suggestions on the chalkboard or an overhead transparency, and have everyone record the guidelines on their sheets. Use the insights and questions below to guide this study.

- **Ecclesiastes 4:9-12.** *Choose friends who will support you.* **Why is this guideline important?** (It's easier to do right when we are not alone in our decisions.)

- **Psalm 34:4.** *Pray.* Just as the Lord took away David's fears when King Saul was trying to kill him, so He can take away our fears when we are being pressured. **What fears might we have at these times?** (Fear of being left out, of losing friends, of being laughed at.)

- **Psalm 46:1.** *Remember God is with you.* **How can remembering this help us when someone is pressuring us?** (God is greater and more powerful than anyone who pressures us to do something wrong or something we don't want to do.)

- **1 Corinthians 10:13.** *God will help you.* **How can this promise help you when your friends want you to do something you don't want to do?** (He gives us the courage and power to say no.)

- **Romans 12:2.** *Suggest alternatives.* J.B. Phillips' translation makes the first part of this verse come alive: "Don't let the world around you squeeze you into its own mold." Decide ahead of time what you will do. **Why is it important to decide ahead of time what you will do in certain circumstances and have alternatives ready to suggest?** (It's easier to make decisions when we're not under pressure. Suggesting alternatives lets our friends know we are not rejecting them personally.) **How can you do this without turning off your friends?** (Say something like this: **"I don't want to do _____, but I still want to be with you. Why don't we do _____ instead.**)

# APPLYING THE TRUTH

### *STUDENT BOOK*

As an option, read one or more of the case studies in the student book chapter. Ask group members what they would do if they were the one being pressured. Then discuss how the guidelines for popping the pressure can be applied in that situation.

## SKITS

Have your group members form the same skit groups as before and choose a pressure one or more of them have experienced recently. Instruct them to act out the situation, showing how the guidelines on the Workout Sheet might help.

Have each group present their skit. As time permits, discuss other possible applications of the guidelines.

## WORKOUT SHEET

Distribute Workout Sheet #18, "Where's Your Pressure Point?" Instruct group members to rate themselves on the pressures listed as well as any others. Then have everyone choose the one on which they rated highest and decide how to deal with it the next time they face it.

## PRAYER

Say something like: **We cannot conquer these pressures in our own strength—at least not for very long. We need to ask for God's help and power. Let's do that right now.** Take time for sentence prayers.

# POP THE PRESSURE



Read each Bible passage, and write a guideline to help you the next time someone pressures you to do something wrong or something you don't want to do.

# WHERE'S YOUR PRESSURE POINT?

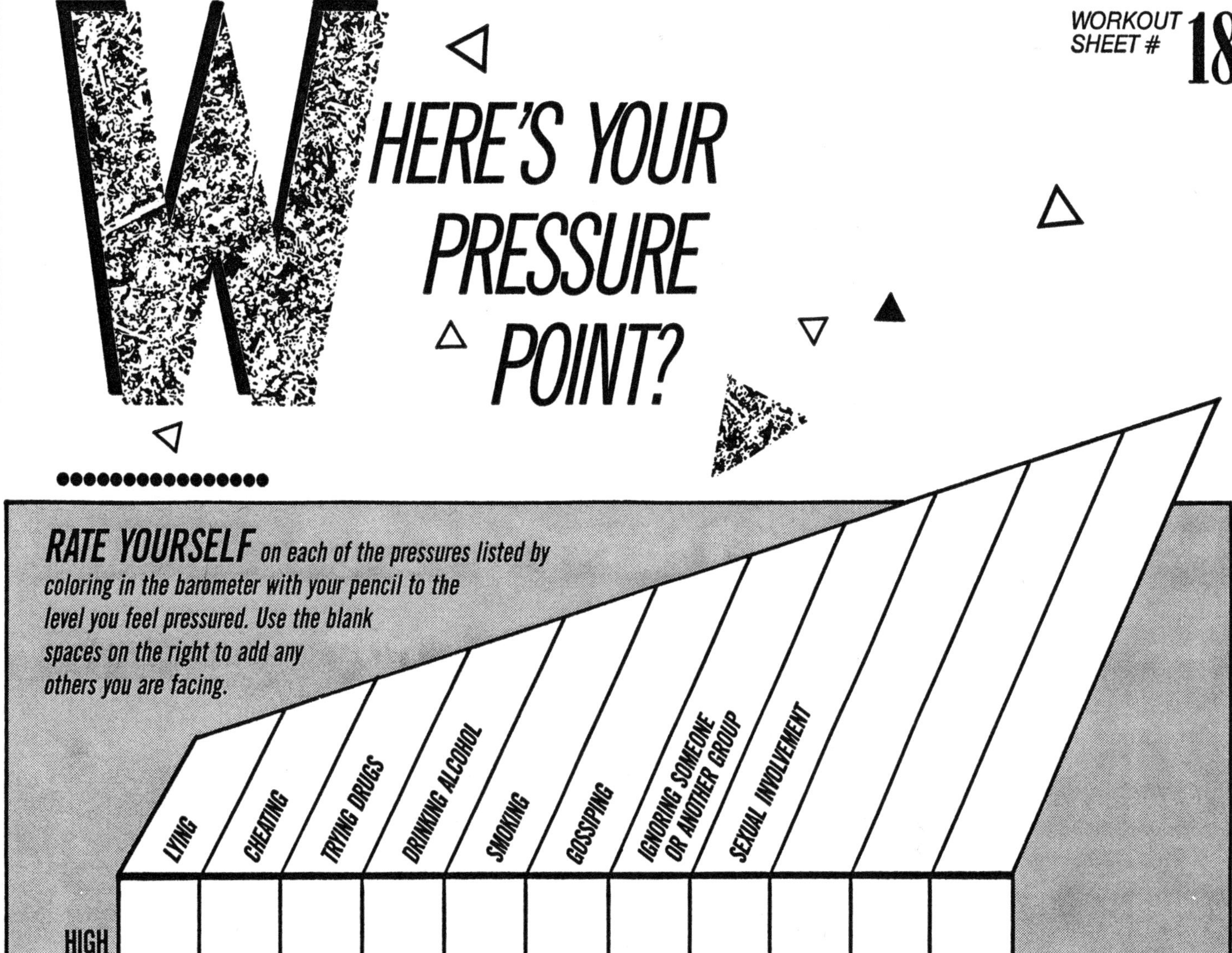


***RATE YOURSELF** on each of the pressures listed by coloring in the barometer with your pencil to the level you feel pressured. Use the blank spaces on the right to add any others you are facing.*

*How can you use the guidelines on Workout Sheet #17 to help you deal with the pressure you rated the highest?*

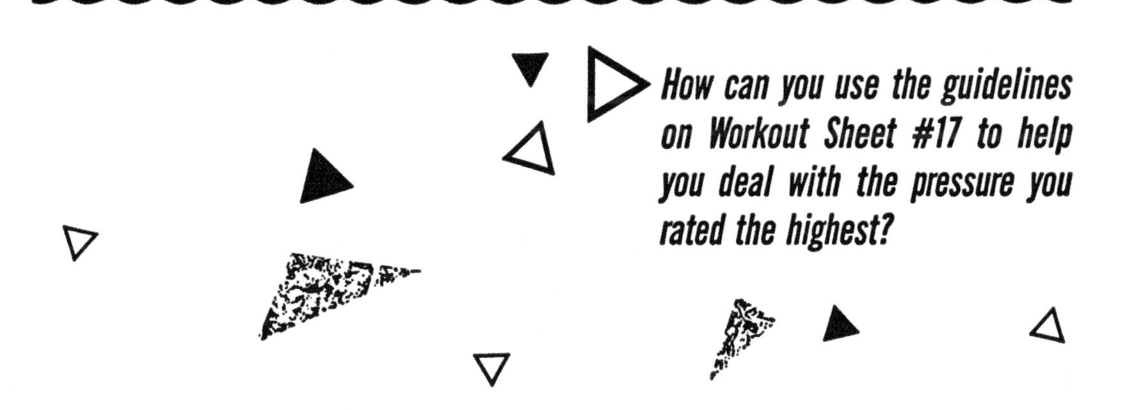

# FRIENDS— OVERCOMING OBSTACLES

*SESSION 10*

# *POPULARITY PROFILE*

**KEY CONCEPT**

Although we are already special to God, popularity with other people is achieved by helping them.

**MEETING THE NEED**

This session will respond to the following student questions and comments:
- "Of course, I want to be liked. Doesn't everybody?"
- "I guess I'm just not popular."
- "I'm tired of being left out all the time."

**SESSION GOALS**

You will help each group member
1. describe a popular person,
2. explore biblical guidelines for popularity and reasons they are already special to God,
3. describe himself and identify ways to use his uniqueness to help other people.

**SPECIAL PREPARATION**

____ Five pieces of wrapped candy or toothpicks for each person for the "I'm Unique" game
____ Tape-record television or radio commercials or locate printed ads. See "Launching the Lesson."
____ Tape player or masking tape
____ Write the Bible references from "Exploring the Word" on sheets of paper, two per sheet.
____ Tape recorders and tapes (optional)

# BUILDING THE BODY

Use one or both of these games to get this session off to an active start.

## *THE POPULARITY GAME*

Explain that you are going to play a game in which popularity will be determined by a number of different standards. Instruct group members to stand up (or sit down) if the statement you read is true of them. Read the introductory phrase with each of the following statements to find out who is popular. Feel free to change the statements to fit your group.

**You are popular if you . . .**
- **are wearing designer jeans**
- **have brown eyes**
- **are exactly 5′ tall**
- **like to help people**
- **belong to a school club**
- **study during study hall**
- **get A's in English or reading class**
- **have long hair**
- **are wearing a watch that is not gold or silver colored**
- **are a cheerleader**
- **own high-top gym shoes**
- **are wearing something blue**
- **are a guy**
- **are a trustworthy friend**
- **are here**

Discuss reactions to the statements.
- **Which popularity standards surprised you?**
- **Which ones didn't you like? Why?**
- **Which ones did you like? Why?**

Some group members probably will express dissatisfaction or frustration with the definitions of popularity, especially the ones they have no control over like brown eyes or height. Point out that what makes people popular changes frequently and varies with the group of people.

## *I'M UNIQUE*

Have group members form groups of four or five. Give each person five small pieces of wrapped candy or toothpicks. Taking turns around the circle, each person should tell something about himself or something he has done which he thinks is not true of anyone else in his group. For example, "I've been white water-rafting" or "I was born in a foreign country." If the statement is not true of the others, they each give him a piece of candy (or toothpick). If it is true of anyone else, those people do not give the teller anything. Play until everyone has had at least two turns. The person with the most objects at the end is the most unique. As a variation, have the most unique from each group face off in a challenge match.

Emphasize that we are all unique and special in spite of how other people judge us and whether or not we're part of the most popular group.

# LAUNCHING THE LESSON

### *TAPED COMMERCIALS OR PRINTED ADS*

Tape-record a number of television or radio commercials for products which promise the users popularity or that they will look or be better. Or collect a number of printed advertisements for the same types of products.

Play your tape, or display the ads by taping them to a wall or the chalkboard. Discuss: **What do these commercials (advertisements) have in common? Can they really do what they say? Why or why not?**

**In spite of what the advertisers want us to believe, using a certain brand of toothpaste, for example, will not automatically make someone popular.**



### *WORKOUT SHEET*

Use Workout Sheet #19 either instead of or in addition to the taped commercials.

If you begin the teaching session with this sheet, introduce it by asking: **What makes a person popular?** (Don't pause to discuss responses now.) **We all have our own definitions of popularity which may or may not be similar.** Refer back to the "Popularity Game" if you played it. **I'd like you to take a few minutes to describe a popular person.**

If you use this Workout Sheet in addition to the commercials, introduce it like this: **Before we look at what the Bible says about popularity, let's describe a popular person.** Distribute Workout Sheet #19, "Pop-Pop-Popularity," and pencils. Instruct everyone to write words or phrases which describe a popular person on the pieces of popcorn illustrated on the sheet. It is not necessary to label every piece.

After a few minutes, call for responses. Note similarities and differences. Say: **Let's see how these compare to the qualities and actions God says are important for popularity.**

# EXPLORING THE WORD

### *MAKING COMMERCIALS*

Divide group members into four groups, appoint leaders, and assign each group two of the following references written on sheets of paper. Instruct them to read their verses and talk about specific ways they can practice these guidelines. Then have each group write a commercial to advertise these teachings. If possible, put each group in a separate room, and have them tape-record their commercial. If not, have each group read it or act it out.

- **Matthew 5:9** (Be a peacemaker.)
- **Mark 10:43** (Be a servant.)
- **Galatians 5:14** (Love others.)
- **Galatians 6:10** (Do good to everyone, especially Christians.)
- **Colossians 1:10** (Please the Lord by the way you live, being fruitful in good works and growing in knowledge about God.)
- **Philippians 2:3-4** (Don't do anything for selfish purposes. Be humble. Put other people before yourself.)
- **Ephesians 4:1-2** (Be humble, gentle, patient, and loving.)
- **Hebrews 13:16** (Do good and share with others.)

After about 20 minutes, reassemble the group and listen to the commercials. Ask group members to compare these discoveries with their previous descriptions of a popular person on the Workout Sheet.



### *STUDENT BOOK OPTION*

As an option, have group members compare God's guidelines for popularity with the way the Bible people in the student book chapter tried to gain it. Discuss together: **In what ways did King Saul, Absalom, and James and John do the opposite of these guidelines?**

- **King Saul:** He was only concerned with himself, wanting to be the most important instead of serving others. When David became more popular, Saul tried to kill him instead of being humble and loving. He certainly wasn't trying to please God with his jealous attitude and actions.
- **Absalom:** Absalom was equally self-serving. Instead of being a peacemaker, he divided the nation in his desire to replace his father David as king. He lied about David instead of trying to do him good and help him. These actions did not please God.
- **James and John:** These two brothers were selfish, thinking of their own honor instead of looking for ways to serve others and do good. Their request shows a definite lack of humility and desire to please God.

### *DISCUSSION*

Ask: **How can following these biblical guidelines make you more popular at school?** Be sure your young teens understand that people, including young teens, like to be with others who are helpful and not concerned about themselves. There will always be some, however, who will not respond as readily to these qualities, but they are the minority.

### *BIBLE SEARCH*

Introduce this next section by saying something like: **There's nothing wrong with wanting to be popular or well-liked as long as we don't**

**compromise biblical standards and we remember that being well-liked by certain people does not equal being better.**

**Even if you are never considered part of the so-called popular groups at school, you are special and important to God for several reasons.** One at a time, have group members turn to the following passages, and ask volunteers to read them aloud. After each reading, ask: **Why are you important to God?**

- **Psalm 139:13-16** (God knew each of us even before our mothers became pregnant. That kind of interest and concern denotes importance.)
- **Genesis 1:27, 31** (God created man in His image and recognized that part of Creation as being good. If we weren't important, He would not have made us like Himself.)

Discuss briefly: **What does it mean to be made in God's image?** Help your young teens to understand that even though we don't look like God physically since He is spirit (John 4:24), we both have intellect, emotions, and will.

- **1 John 4:9-10** (God loves us so much that He sent His only Son to die for our sins so we can spend eternity with Him. He would not have paid such a high price if we were not important to Him.)

### *DISCUSSION*

Discuss together: **How does knowing you are special and important to God make you feel? How does it change your definition of a popular person?**

Do not rush over this discussion. Young teens tend to live by their feelings, so it is important that they begin to feel special to God. Emphasize that no matter how other people treat them, they are still important to God.

# APPLYING THE TRUTH

### *WORKOUT SHEET*

Distribute Workout Sheet #20, "One-of-a-Kind." Help your group members to celebrate their own specialness by making a personal coat of arms according to the directions. Explain that a coat of arms is an important way of identifying families and individuals in some countries.

Also instruct everyone to write several ways they can use their uniqueness to follow the biblical guidelines for popularity they studied earlier in this session. Emphasize again that true popularity which lasts comes from helping other people.

## PRAYER

Take a few minutes for sentence prayers, encouraging everyone to thank God for one aspect of their uniqueness and to ask Him for help to use that to serve someone else.

P-P-P-P-POPULARITY
Our popularity popper is cooking up another popular person. What is he or she like? What makes him/her popular? Write one word or phrase on these pieces of popcorn.

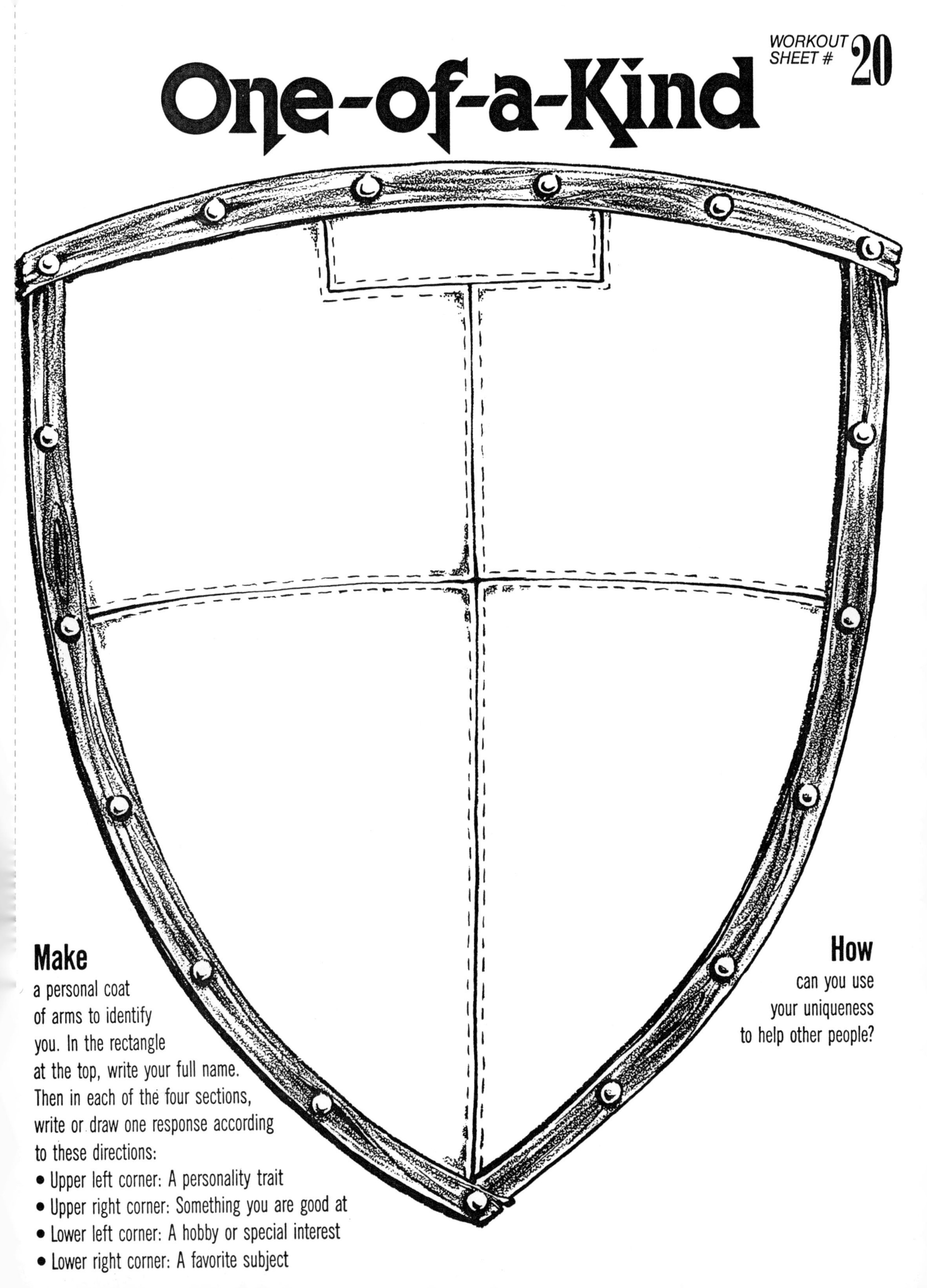
WORKOUT SHEET # 20
One-of-a-Kind
Make
a personal coat
of arms to identify
you. In the rectangle
at the top, write your full name.
Then in each of the four sections,
write or draw one response according
to these directions:
• Upper left corner: A personality trait
• Upper right corner: Something you are good at
• Lower left corner: A hobby or special interest
• Lower right corner: A favorite subject
How
can you use
your uniqueness
to help other people?

# FRIENDS—OVERCOMING OBSTACLES

*SESSION 11*

# CLIMBING THE WALLS

**KEY CONCEPT**

We need to identify and overcome barriers to friendships.

**MEETING THE NEED**

This session will respond to the following student questions and comments:

- "What do you do when you get so mad at one of your friends that you feel like strangling her?"
- "I hate it when I find out one of my friends lied to me or about me."
- "I don't like it when my friends brag about having something I don't have."

**SESSION GOALS**

You will help each group member

1. identify obstacles that get in the way of friendships,
2. explore ways to overcome friendship barriers,
3. choose one way to begin to overcome an obstacle in his or her friendships.

**SPECIAL PREPARATION**

___ If you use the "Obstacle Course Relay," collect objects to design at least two identical obstacle courses.
___ Think of a fight you had with a friend, and be prepared to tell your group about it.
___ Make enough bricks out of construction paper for everyone to have one, plus a few extra for visitors.
___ Marking pens, enough for everyone
___ Masking tape
___ Write the obstacles and corresponding Bible references from the "Bible Study" on separate slips of paper.

# BUILDING THE BODY

Use one or both of these games to start your session in an active way and to introduce the subject of obstacles that get in the way of friendships.

### *OBSTACLE COURSE*

Using such objects as boxes, tires, tables, chairs, nets, and whatever else you can find, set up two identical obstacle courses of five to seven challenges in a room or outdoors. Design your course so half of the obstacles lead away from the starting point and half lead back to it. Challenges might include jumping over a box, running through four tires, ducking under a table, climbing to a low branch on a tree and back down, riding a tricycle to the next challenge.



Divide your group into two teams, and explain the obstacle course route and requirements. Have pairs from each team run a relay through their course, helping each other if necessary. The next pair cannot start until both of the previous pair return to the starting line. If you have an odd number of teens on a team, ask one person to participate twice. The first team to finish wins.

### *HUMAN OBSTACLES*

Divide your group into four teams, and assign each team a corner of the room. The object of the game is for each team to move in a designated manner to the corner which is diagonal from them. The first team to get to the opposite corner wins that round. Before giving the "go" signal for the round, announce the manner in which teams must cross the room. For example, instruct them to walk backwards, to hop, to roll, to pair up as wheelbarrows and drivers, to skip, etc. When the teams cross in the center, they will encounter a lot of human obstacles! The team which wins the most rounds is the winner.

# LAUNCHING THE LESSON

### *STUDENT BOOK OPTION*

Read aloud the section in the student book entitled "What Kind of Builder Are You?" Ask several volunteers to describe a fight with a friend without using names. Then share one of your own fights. Point out that we all have to deal with obstacles that come between friends.

### *GRAFFITI BRICKS*

Give everyone a paper brick and a marking pen. Instruct them to write a word or short phrase on the brick which completes this sentence: **It's hard to be friends with someone when he or she ______.** When individuals finish the sentence, have them tape their bricks on a wall to form a paper wall. Read all the answers aloud.

Point out that most friendships run into barriers like these at one time or another. In today's session you will study seven common obstacles and how to overcome them in order to remain friends.

# EXPLORING THE WORD

## *WORKOUT SHEET*

Distribute Workout Sheet #21, "Alien Attack," and pencils. Instruct group members to use the Bible verses in the decoder bank to identify the obstacles which come between friends and write the correct name on each rock. Note that the exact word may not be in the verse. Answers are:

- Slessenfish—selfishness, James 3:14
- Tricicims—criticism, Proverbs 12:18
- Veny—envy, Galatians 5:26
- Driep—pride, Proverbs 13:10
- Narge—anger, Proverbs 29:22
- Gliny—lying, Proverbs 26:28
- Sopsig—gossip, Proverbs 16:28

When everyone is finished, call for reports. Then briefly discuss how each can ruin a friendship. Remind group members that it isn't always the other person who raises these barriers; sometimes it's us.

## *BIBLE STUDY*

Make a transition into the next activity by saying something like: **Now that we've identified some common attacks on friendships, let's look at God's counterattacks.**

Distribute slips of paper with the following obstacles and corresponding Bible references to individuals, pairs, or small groups. Instruct them to read the verse and pick out how we are to respond to that obstacle from someone else or to keep from doing it ourselves. Write their answers on the chalkboard or an overhead transparency next to the barrier. Use the questions below to discuss ways to practice God's instructions as reports are given. Push group members to be specific.

- Selfishness—Philippians 2:3-4
  **How can we put other people's interests before our own?**
- Criticism—Matthew 7:1
  **How can we obey God's command not to judge or criticize another person?**
- Envy—1 Timothy 6:6-8
  **How does contentment counteract envy or jealousy?**
- Pride—Romans 12:3, 16
  **What helps us not to think more highly of ourselves than we should?**

- Anger—James 1:19
  **How does listening and not speaking right away help us control anger?**
- Lying—Ephesians 4:25
  **What can help us to speak truth instead of lies?**
- Gossip—Proverbs 11:13
  **What can help us keep secrets?**

### SUMMARY

Have everyone look at 1 Corinthians 13:4-6. Ask group members to choose the description of love in these verses which counteracts each obstacle that gets in the way of our friendships. Suggestions are:



- Selfishness—not self-seeking
- Criticism—kind, keeps no record of wrongs
- Envy—does not envy
- Pride—does not boast, not proud
- Anger—patient, not easily angered
- Lying—rejoices with the truth
- Gossip—kind, always protects, trusts

Point out that if we are practicing love, we will not be erecting barriers between us and other people.

Summarize this study by having a volunteer read Luke 6:31. Ask: **How will obedience to this command help us to keep our friends?** (If we treat them like we want to be treated, we will not let any of these obstacles get in the way.)

# APPLYING THE TRUTH

### WORKOUT SHEET

Distribute Workout Sheet #22, "Barrier Buster." Have each group member choose the barrier which gets in the way of his friendships most often and lightly shade the brick. If it is not written on the wall, he should write it on one of the blank bricks. Then have everyone write on the wrecking ball one thing he will begin doing to help "smash" that barrier. Have those who wrote in barriers use their Bible concordances to find verses to help them.

### PRAYER

Have a time of sentence prayers focusing on practicing what they studied in this session in order to be better friends.

# ALIEN ATTACK

***Below are seven obstacles which get in the way of friendships. With the help of the Bible verses in the decoder bank, unscramble the words to find out what they are and write the correct spelling underneath.***

• GLINY •

• SLESSENFISH •

• SOPSIG •

• TRICICIMS •

• DRIEP •

• VENY •

• NARGE •

## DECODER BANK

Proverbs 12:18
Proverbs 13:10
Proverbs 16:28
Proverbs 26:28
Proverbs 29:22
Galatians 5:26
James 3:14

# BARRIER BUSTER

Pick out the barrier with which you have the most trouble in your friendships. Lightly shade that brick below. If it is not on the wall, write it on one of the blank bricks. Then choose one specific way you will begin to "smash" that barrier, and write it on the wrecking ball.

SELFISHNESS

CRITICISM

JEALOUSY

ANGER

LYING

GOSSIP

PRIDE

# FRIENDS— OVERCOMING OBSTACLES

## *SESSION 12*

# *WHEN FRIENDS FIGHT*

**KEY CONCEPT**

Conflicts don't have to break up friends.

**MEETING THE NEED**

This session will respond to the following student questions and comments:

- "I hate it when my friends talk about activities I'm not invited to."
- "The biggest problem I have with my friends is not agreeing on everything."
- "What do I do when my friend and I want to do different things but neither of us will give in?"

**SESSION GOALS**

You will help each group member
1. identify a conflict with a friend,
2. discover biblical guidelines for solving conflicts with others,
3. role play how to solve conflicts with friends.

**SPECIAL PREPARATION**

____ Bring two 3′ ropes or strips of sturdy cloth for "Friend Relay Race."
____ Locate a tape with the song "Even the Best of Friends" by Randy Stonehill (on his tape *Equator,* published by Myrrh), and bring a cassette player.
____ Make a transparency or poster of Workout Sheet #24, and bring an appropriate marking pen.

# BUILDING THE BODY

Use one or both of the following games to get this session off to an active start.

### FRIEND TAG

Have everyone pair off and put their arms around each other's waist. (If possible, it's probably better to have them pair off by sex.) Designate one pair as "It," and play tag. When the It pair tags another couple, they become It, etc. Caution group members that they must stay locked with their partners at all times.

When time is up, talk about how difficult it was to stay together and still play the game reasonably well.

### FRIEND RELAY RACE

Divide your group into two teams, and have each team form a straight line facing the finish line. Have the first two people on each team stand side by side, and tie together the two legs nearest each other with a piece of rope or a cloth strip. On your signal to go, each pair races to the finish line and back. When they return to their team, they remove the rope and tie up the next two people who run the relay race. Continue until one team has completed the relay.

Briefly discuss the difficulties team members had in running this relay.

# LAUNCHING THE LESSON

### SONG

Play the song "Even the Best of Friends" by Randy Stonehill.

**What does this song teach about friendships?** (Even best friends have conflicts. If they are going to remain friends, they have to learn to give in, forgive, and love each other.)

### STUDENT BOOK OPTION

Have two group members read or act out the dialogue between Tony and Ken at the beginning of the chapter in the student book. Use this conflict to get your teens thinking about their own fights in preparation for completing Workout Sheet #23.

### *WORKOUT SHEET*

Distribute Workout Sheet #23, "The Big Fight," and pencils. Instruct everyone to think of a fight they had with a friend. Using the following questions, guide group members to fill in the plot summary.

- Scene: **What did you fight about?**
- Motivation: **Why?**
- Dialogue & Actions: **What did you say? How did you act?**
- Feelings: Me: **How did you feel?**
  My friend: **How do you think your friend felt?**

Ask volunteers to describe their fights without naming the friend. If your group is small, you may want to go around the circle and have everyone respond. Or collect all the sheets, shuffle them, distribute them, and have everyone read the one he received. (It doesn't matter if someone gets his own; no one else will know.)

Summarize by pointing out that we all have fights with our friends. But these conflicts don't have to break up friendships if we follow God's guidelines for solving our differences.



# EXPLORING THE WORD

### *BIBLE STUDY*

Ask a volunteer to briefly review the relationship between Paul and Barnabas. (See session #7.) Then have group members read Acts 15:36-40. Discuss the following questions, using the information in parentheses to supplement group members' answers.

- **What did Paul and Barnabas fight about? Why?** (Barnabas wanted to take John Mark along on their second missionary journey, but Paul disagreed because Mark had deserted them on the first journey. Barnabas may have been willing to give Mark a second chance because they were cousins [Colossians 4:10] and/or he recognized Mark's potential even though he had failed the first time. Also Barnabas was called the Son of Encouragement [Acts 4:36], and he may have thought he could encourage Mark by taking him on another journey.)

- **Who was right?** (It's interesting that Luke reports this conflict without assigning blame to either party. Sometimes two people can disagree and neither one is wrong.)

- **How did they solve their disagreement?** (They each went in separate directions, Barnabas with John Mark and Paul with Silas. Sometimes—but not often—it's necessary for friends to part, but there are ways to patch up disagreements which you will study shortly.)

Have group members read the following verses. Ask what each one tells us about Paul's later relationship with John Mark.

- **Colossians 4:10-11** (Mark worked with Paul and was a comfort to him.)
- **Philemon 24** (Again Paul mentioned that John Mark was a fellow worker.)
- **2 Timothy 4:11** (Paul wrote this book from prison shortly before he was killed. He wanted Mark to come to him because Mark was helpful to him in his ministry.)

Summarize: **The Bible doesn't tell us when or how Paul changed his mind about John Mark, but it's obvious Mark grew spiritually under his cousin's guidance.**

## *WORKOUT SHEET*



Say something like: **The Bible does give us guidelines for solving conflicts with other people, some of which Paul probably used. Let's look at them.**

Distribute Workout Sheet #24, "The Path to Solving Conflicts," and assign each of the nine Scripture references to individuals, pairs, or small groups. Instruct them to read the verses and record the step(s) to take to solve a conflict with a friend.

When everyone is finished, call for reports. As the steps are given, have each group member complete his Workout Sheet. You may want to make a transparency or poster of this sheet to fill out as group members report. Use the following commentary and questions to supplement responses.

- **Luke 6:37** (Don't judge or condemn your friend. You may not know all the facts behind his or her behavior. Instead, be forgiving.)
- **Proverbs 17:9** (Sometimes we just need to overlook the offense and forget it. A lot of our conflicts are the result of personality differences which are not going to change; therefore, we need to learn to accept people as they are.)
- **Colossians 3:13** (Bearing with each other means to put up with or hold back instead of getting mad or retaliating. Also we are to forgive as the Lord forgave us.) Ask: **How has the Lord forgiven us?** (Completely and unconditionally.)
- **Matthew 5:23-24** (We are to take the first step toward being friends again even if we are not at fault. This is hard to do! But God will help us if we ask Him.)
- **Ephesians 4:15, 25, 29** (We are to speak the truth in love. Sometimes this includes pointing out sinful actions but always with the attitude of helping the other person, not criticizing him or her.)
- **Ephesians 4:26-27, 31** (It's OK to be angry, but we need to clear up the conflict that makes us angry as soon as possible instead of holding a grudge.)
- **Ephesians 4:32** (We are to be kind and compassionate and forgiving

just like God is with us.)

- **1 John 4:19-21** (Love the other person instead of hating him or her.) Ask: **How do we obey this command in practical ways when we've had a fight with someone?** (Don't stop being friends. Follow the rest of these guidelines to resolve the fight.)

- **Matthew 18:21-22** (Forgive more than once if necessary. Keep on forgiving.)

# APPLYING THE TRUTH

## *ROLE PLAYS*

Divide group members into small groups of three to six. Instruct each group to choose one fight from Workout Sheet #23, or give each group one sheet as their assignment. Have each group talk about alternate responses to the conflict based on the guidelines recorded on Workout Sheet #24. Each group should then choose two people to role play the situation for the rest of the group to demonstrate how to practice biblical principles in everyday situations.

After each group has presented their role play, discuss other responses as time permits.

## *PRAYER*

Have a few minutes of silent prayer. Encourage group members to talk to God about any unresolved fights they have had with their friends, asking for His forgiveness where they were wrong and for His help to do what they can to become friends again. Close with audible prayer.

## *EVALUATION*

If you used all twelve of these lesson plans for a continuous study, instead of breaking them into three units, take a few minutes to evaluate with your group. Ask your young teens to respond verbally or in writing to some or all of the following questions:

- **What did you like best about this study on friendship?**
- **What did you like least?**
- **How has this study helped you?**
- **What one thing (i.e., content, activity, assignment) helped you the most?**

Think of a fight you've had with a friend. How would you describe that fight if you were writing a story or movie scene about it?

▶ **CAST OF CHARACTERS:**

*Friend*

*Me*

▶ **SCENE:**

▶ **MOTIVATION:**

▶ **DIALOGUE & ACTIONS.**

▶ **FEELINGS:**

*Friend:*

*Me:*

WORKOUT SHEET # 24
THE PATH TO SOLVING CONFLICTS
The Bible offers helpful steps to resolving conflicts. How many of them can you find in the Scriptures found on this footpath?
Your Friend
CON-FLICTS RESOLVED
Matthew 18:21-22
1 John 4:19-21
Ephesians 4:32
Ephesians 4:26-27, 31
Ephesians 4:15, 25, 29
Matthew 5:23-24
Colossians 3:13
Proverbs 17:9
Luke 6:37
START
You

# FRIENDS—WHO NEEDS THEM?

## EVALUATION SHEET

**Dear Leader,**
You can have a real impact on future Young Teen Feedback Electives! Please take a minute to fill out this form giving us your candid reaction to this material. Thanks for your help.

***ABOUT YOU***
In what setting did you use this elective? (Sunday School, youth group, midweek Bible study, etc.)

______________________________________________

How many young people were in your group? ______________________

What was the age-range of those in your group? ______________________

How many weeks did you spend on this study? ______________________

How long was your average meeting time? ______________________

(Optional) Name ______________________

Address ______________________

***ABOUT THIS YOUNG TEEN FEEDBACK ELECTIVE***
Did you and your young people enjoy this study? (Why or why not?)

What are the strengths and weaknesses of this leader's book?

Did you use the student books? _____ Yes _____ No
If so, what are their strengths and weaknesses?

***ABOUT THE FUTURE***
What topics and issues would you like to see covered in future electives?

What Bible studies would you like to see included in future electives?

Do you plan to use other Young Teen Feedback Electives? (Why or why not?)

Do you plan to repeat this study in the future with new students? (Why or why not?)

Place
stamp
here

**SonPower Youth Sources Editor**
1825 College Avenue
Wheaton, Illinois 60187